# Lee Prosser

# Midwest Hauntings

4880 Lower Valley Road, Atglen, Pennsylvania 19310

Disclaimer: Many of the locations and settings in this book are open to the public. Others are on private property, or condemned for safety reasons. I urge you not to trespass on private property. Please have respect for the current owners and their ghosts. Any area that is posted "No Trespassing" means just that, and trespassers can be and often are prosecuted. Don't take chances with your life and well-being, or those of your friends. Get permission to investigate and explore before you do it. You will be glad you did.

Schiffer Books are available at special discounts for bulk purchases for sales promotions or premiums. Special editions, including personalized covers, corporate imprints, and excerpts can be created in large quantities for special needs. For more information contact the publisher:

Published by Schiffer Publishing Ltd.
4880 Lower Valley Road
Atglen, PA 19310
Phone: (610) 593-1777;
Fax: (610) 593-2002
E-mail: Info@schifferbooks.com

For the largest selection of fine reference books on this and related subjects, please visit our web site at:
**www.schifferbooks.com**
We are always looking for people to write books on new and related subjects. If you have an idea for a book please contact us at the above address.

This book may be purchased from the publisher.
Include $5.00 for shipping.
Please try your bookstore first.
You may write for a free catalog.

In Europe, Schiffer books are distributed by
Bushwood Books
6 Marksbury Ave.
Kew Gardens
Surrey TW9 4JF England
Phone: 44 (0) 20 8392 8585; Fax: 44 (0) 20 8392 9876
E-mail: info@bushwoodbooks.co.uk
Website: www.bushwoodbooks.co.uk

Cover photo: Corn Field at Sunset © Tony Campbell. *Courtesy of bigstockphoto.com.*

# Contents

# Acknowledgments

† To my wife Debra, whose inspiration, humor, and encouragement is an ongoing joy, for which I thank her!

† To my daughters, their husbands, and children with love.

† To the following friends for various reasons: Jeff Belanger, Gerina Dunwich, Don Bachardy, Alina Ivanova, Russell and Mary Wlodek, Jerry L. Anderson, Ray Bradbury, John Truett, Morrice Blackwell, Paulinho Garcia, Alice V. Spencer, Bob and Jane McHugh, Gene M. Gressley, Dan Farkas, Devadatta Kali, and Terry Kelly who painted "Enchanted Desert." May each of you be blessed with joy, humor, good health, peace, and happiness.

† To my wonderful editors, Jennifer Marie Savage and Dinah Roseberry, for their input and support.

# PREFACE

In writing about ghosts, paranormal and supernatural themes, UFOs, the unknown, and the strange, it is always enjoyable to keep in mind that there is so much information about it that a writer will never run out of material or sources to investigate! As long as people talk and share stories and record what they have encountered, then there will be knowledge to shed light upon these topics. Historical documentation is found everywhere, and one of the fun resources is digging into old newspapers.

When I write my column, "Bide One's Time," for Ghostvillage. com, I am always amazed by the response, inquiries, and comments from readers. The more people share and read about the unknown, the less unknown the unknown becomes! I wonder as I wander through the many pathways that take me on a trip down some direction — and sometimes that trip is a truly macabre journey.

It is my goal with this book to share with you, the readers, everything I came across in the haunted Heartland. It is not my role to disprove or prove these paranormal occurrences, but to share them. I hope you enjoy reading this book as much as I did in writing it.

## Introduction
# THE HAUNTED HEARTLAND

    The Heartland of the United States, known as the Midwest, contains a wide diversity of hauntings and includes the following states: *Kansas, Michigan, Minnesota, Illinois, Indiana, Iowa, Missouri, Nebraska, North Dakota, South Dakota, Ohio, and Wisconsin*.

    Although there are often better known paranormal and haunting occurrences in the big and small cities, it is because there are more people to witness them and the memories of such events tend to linger from one group to another. However, in small, isolated areas, there are also such events that take place or have taken place. The simple fact is, each is remembered in some form of expression.

UFO sightings and monster encounters are among the many things these states have in common, and each state will intrigue readers for different reasons. As you will soon discover, each state is exciting in its own right — and each state has a wide range of ghostly hauntings and paranormal experiences.

Independent research will also turn up a wide gathering of paranormal activity. There is much that can be found in your local library and newspaper morgue for information and stories that sometimes do not make news outside of the region in which they took place.

People, too, are your greatest asset when investigating the unknown. For instance, you may come across a man whose great aunt had an encounter with a ghost at such and such a place. Well, that aunt may be dead, and the story old, but chances are that ghost is still where it was last encountered! Don't be afraid to question, query, and ask about hauntings. Most people do not what to share some family paranormal experiences because it is embarrassing to them, and there can be a sense of stigma attached to such stories. Respect their privacy, but follow up the best way you can and see what happens in your investigation. There is always something that will turn up. Privacy and trust between a ghost investigator and the people involved is of utmost importance. There are ghost stories and hauntings out there waiting to be analyzed and written about. Go find them and enjoy the journey along the way to discovery!

# UFOs

Unidentified Flying Objects, or UFOs, is something bound to stir up controversy anywhere in the world. The United States, like every other nation, has its share of reliable documented sightings. In many instances, there are actual encounters with extraterrestrials and incidents of abductions of humans by extraterrestrials.

I have seen UFOs, either by myself, with my wife Debra, or in the company of friends over the many decades, but rather than experiencing a sense of fear, instead I have experienced an ongoing sense of curiosity. I am an inquisitive man, and I am curious about the paranormal, occult, and UFO happenings. My interest started when I was a child, at which time my late uncle, Willard David Firestone,

guided me in the proper channels. What he showed me, explained, and shared helped shape my investigative nature into examining all meaningful things found in the unknown. Of course, some things were more meaningful than others.

I learned to discern between the fake and the real. I did not set out to disprove or to prove, but to document those paranormal and UFO situations I encountered during my life. I did not hesitate to expose something I thought was a fake, and I did not hesitate to document something I knew was true. The truth is really out there for everyone to discover, and all each of us has to do is look hard for it and come to understand its reason for being the way it happens to be.

Also, it is fair to state that throughout the history of humankind one person's encounter may be another's vision and may also be another's prophecy, and still yet, another's gospel, delusion, or fantasy! To explain humankind in an existential perspective: We are what we do and we do what we are. Humans usually try to make sense out of situations even if they do not know exactly what they are doing, but they do usually muddle through and uncover some meaningful truth. To question, observe, document, and witness is what a paranormal investigator does, and that certainly includes encounters with the UFO phenomena.

Unidentified flying objects have been with us since we became a viable species on earth, and whatever mutations and alterations to us that were made and continue to be made by extraterrestrials is what we have come to, this day in time and place. Each of us has gifts and those gifts were and remain our natural trademark by birth, a gift from the Creator. They have also in subtle ways been augmented and developed along certain positive paths by extraterrestrials.

By whatever appearance or form these beings may be, I believe the majority of them seek to help us develop into citizens of the universe, although there are some who would mutate us into exotic food stock or slaves. There are more and more contacts taking place now, since the decade of the 1990s, than ever before. There is coming a time when organized governments of the planet earth will no longer be able to cover-up or underplay so-called alien influences involved in the human race. Put aside the call for a new world order and look around you: the new world order of control governments seek is not the world order of extraterrestrial peace and positive living. That the human spirit is capable of great heroic deeds and generosity becomes more evident as times become more complex and governments become more intense in their efforts to reach out and control all human activities, feelings, and dreams. Those of you who have read the classic novel, *Brave New World* by Aldous Huxley, should well remember what governments do to humans!

What is one to do, the question is asked? Rely on your intuition and not on the false promises of world governments whose sole purpose is to ensure their ongoing control and absolute power over the people they were originally established to protect. To look within oneself and see the light of truth is forever more valid than accepting the word of politicians as absolute truth. Look within and listen to what your intuition tells you — or you can follow the sheep herd and conclude your life by being castrated in one form or another, sheared of all your covering and chopped up as packaged meat for food consumption.

Based on what I have encountered over the many years, I believe that extraterrestrials as a whole mean humans no harm and would like to see humans' progress and develop into a species ready to be part of a universe of peaceful ways. There are, however, some extraterrestrial groups that would enslave humans for personal reasons, peculiar to their individual needs.

In the meantime, we endure, and we go on. The human race must endure; anything after that is secondary. Once we secure our position, the human race can become what it is destined to become and become part of the intergalactic community as an individual species capable of great accomplishments through its own individuality. We are not alone in the universe. We have never been alone.

Further, there is ongoing debate over the connection of certain aspects of paranormal and extraterrestrial activities. To find certain links, each of us has to be cautious and look beyond the oftentimes seemingly obvious. When it comes to analyzing happenings of the paranormal and the extraterrestrial, there is always something there that goes beyond the obvious. The truth and possible connection has to be viewed, documented, and discussed. Some happenings are ghostly and paranormal. Some happenings are extraterrestrial. Some have possible elements of both. It is up to each of us to discern the differences where they exist and write and talk about them.

# TIME PORTALS AND THE PARANORMAL

Time portals and the paranormal are topics that will intrigue, fascinate, scare, and confound people. They are not new topics, but are topics open to change and ongoing revelation of facts. For the most part, much of the documentation is true and some is not; however, to the world at large, they remain simply unproven topics of books, movies, writings, and convention talk! To the world at large, the open acceptance of the topic of time portals is unacceptable although by its very nature time portals would explain many occurrences over the past several thousand years that fit into its analysis.

I have never thought the idea of one dimension or two dimensions or three dimensions satisfactorily explains the unexplained! I believe there is a fourth dimension, and probably additional dimensions the human mind is not yet able to embrace and understand in a meaningful manner. Look at the marvelous tinkering that has been done to humans since they were found able to withstand those tinkerings, and look what has become of us as a race of sentient beings upon the planet Earth! Look at what humankind has achieved in its most recent past, say, the last one hundred years. Look past the wars and religious strife and silliness, and examine the achievements. Yes, we are what we do and we do what we are. There are reasons why we have been allowed to survive as a race, and one important factor is the outside influence of beings more developed than we are, and those beings know what they are doing.

If you get to the heart of the matter and re-examine the concept of The Rapture, then you have to realize this is not necessarily a religious intervention, but instead, something akin to a spiritual awakening of the mind with cleared perceptions. It is logically possible that this is the work of a much more advanced humanity from our future working with various races of extraterrestrials. This is an option for consideration, one that is truer than we dare know! I have read, heard about, personally encountered, and been told of encounters with time portals since I was a child in the 1950s, and with the passage of time, I have correlated them into a collection of information that tells me in an honest, straight-forward manner — time portals do exist, you have encountered contact with them more frequently than you realize or remember as has most of humankind, and such activity with these time portals will continue to become more prevalent and openly occurring in the years ahead!

Don't be afraid of time portal contacts. Remember if it comes to you, it is because there is a defined reason for it doing so; accept it as such and go on. To foolishly dismiss the idea of time portal contact is to dismiss the idea that the very roots of our humanity grow and spread out in wonderful ways in which we are not fully aware of the consequences. If we accept the possibility that each of us is a spiritual being and realize we are not alone in the universe, those trying to help us via way of extraterrestrial or advanced human guidance will find a way to reach us in a positive manner best suited to each human contactee.

This applies to what may lie behind many paranormal occurrences, or what humans perceive as paranormal occurrences, which include several types of hauntings. Have you ever stopped to consider that the images of historical figures and loved ones haunting our imaginations and existences are there via way of intelligent and residual hauntings... there for a specific reason and at a specific time to remind us of something we need to know and recall? Anything is possible in the world of the unknown, the paranormal, sentient beings from other dimensions, and extraterrestrials from inner and outer space. It is up to each of us to encounter and find that something we need to know and recall. We can and we will. Again, we are what we do and we do what we are. Humanity is on the verge of becoming what it is envisioned to be and it will survive. Those survivors will be like nothing ever seen before on planet Earth. As to alternate universes, why not! I certainly believe in the possibility of their existence. I would like to think that in an alternate universe, the *Titanic* did sail into port at New York and was never sunk by an iceberg. I think it is interesting to consider other such situations. Of course, people will think up many, many such situations of their own personal design. Here are a few — each one has its own food for thought!

- How would it have been if Senator Robert F. Kennedy had gone on to win the United States Presidency? Likewise, what would have happened if President John Kennedy had never entered politics or been elected?

- What if President Nixon had never become involved in Watergate and had never been forced to resign from office?

- What if Reagan and Bush, both George and George W., had never been elected Presidents?

- What if The Beatles, Queen, Judy Garland, The Beach Boys, Cole Porter, Frank Sinatra, George Gershwin, Ella Fitzgerald, Elvis Presley, Johnny Cash, Barbra Streisand, and Prince had never pursued music careers?

- What if Stephen King, John Steinbeck, H. G. Wells, and Ernest Hemingway had never become writers?

- What if the bombing of Pearl Harbor had never taken place?

- What if Adolph Hitler was never born?

- What if World Wars One and Two had never taken place?

- What would have happened if the American Indians never had their land stolen from them and genocide of entire tribes had never taken place?

In the realm of alternate universes, those situations could actually have happened that way. Is it science fiction, fantasy, or horror? Are such things possible? Could a time line be successfully altered while remaining unaltered in another line, and how many times can such an alteration be achieved? For instance, do the highly respected Academy Award winners Katherine Hepburn and Gary Cooper still exist in other time lines, or is ours the only one they are known as actors in? Perhaps each was a dentist in another alternate universe on a different time line! What if movies do not exist in other alternate universes, and they are not part of any time line anywhere! Re-read William Shakespeare's play, *Hamlet*, and see how that perspective fits into the scope of alternate universes. You may be surprised the more you consider what Shakespeare was saying. There really is more out there to consider and wonder about than we know!

## About Orbs

Orbs are round balls of light that are directly connected to spirit energy. Though they come in different colors, orbs are usually white. It would be interesting and informative if more paranormal investigators would name the color of the orbs they encounter in their writings; by sharing this data, you can get a feel and understanding of the importance of orbs.

Over the years, I have found that white orbs are associated with healing. Other orbs are associated with individual colors. There are many books available on color, color magick, applications of color therapy in healing, biblical and occult color associations, and paranormal orbs and their meanings and through them you will see how certain colors identify an orb you come into contact with during your paranormal investigations.

Although orbs are most often witnessed in cemeteries, or at gravesites, they can appear anywhere and at any time. Orbs can appear in your bedroom at night or in the day, or in different locations within a home or a building, including stairwells and elevators. If you can see the color, then you are able to more readily understand what type of spirit energy is connected with that orb.

# Chapter One:
# Kansas

A battle ground during the American Civil War, Kansas is also an area of weather extremes with a history of paranormal activity.

With its capital Topeka and its largest city Wichita, admission to the United States as a state came January 29, 1861. A Native American tribe named the Kansa originally inhabited this state, and the name of the state's most famous river is named after them and known as the Kansas River; one of the prevalent nicknames of the river is the Kaw. An interesting historical note about the Kansa Tribe is its colorful mystical name, "people of the wind." Today the state of Kansas is a thriving place with a rich, colorful past.

At this time, there are twenty-three national landmarks in Kansas, including the Hollenberg Pony Express Station State Historic Site, Marais des Cygnes Massacre State Historical Site, the Carry A. Nation House, Shawnee Indian Mission State Historical Site, and the Nicodemus Historic District.

There are many famous people connected with the state of Kansas, including Jane Grant, Karl Menninger, Amelia Earhart, Dwight D. Eisenhower, Gale Sayers, Gordon Parks, Buster Keaton, Robert J. Dole, John Brown, Stan Kenton, Wyatt Earp, Frederic Remington, Dee Wallace Stone, Rex Stout, Eva Jessye, and Gwendolyn Brooks.

## Stull

Originally called Deer Creek Community, historical data reveals the name was changed to that of the first postmaster, whose name was Sylvester Stull, during the summer of 1899. This city has had macabre stories written about its area and its peculiar cemetery, Stull Cemetery, for over thirty years.

Stories of devil worship have been told in regard to the history of this old Kansas cemetery. If you are curious about this place, it should be noted that it is posted "No Trespassing" and is now on private property. Visitors are not welcome there, as many various reports have stated over the years.

Stull Cemetery is located near the northwestern corner of Clinton Lake, approximately ten miles west of Lawrence, Kansas. The legends and paranormal encounters surrounding this area and its now destroyed old church are complex. A story about UFOs in the cemetery area during the late 1980s has been talked about in different circles. The remnants of the original church are scatted about the cemetery, mostly confined to one area where shadow figures are said to dance in and around its ruins during the twilight hours.

For over 130 years there have been stories of Witch torturing and hangings at this cemetery, where male Witches were hanged by the testicles and then beaten to death, where strange unearthly winds howl with ill odors against those who would dare enter the cemetery grounds, where strange deaths have taken place and never explained, and tales of demon children playing in the west side of the cemetery. Appearances of the devil are told frequently.

People are advised not to go near this macabre cemetery setting during the night hours; however, continuing scare stories have turned this cemetery into a most unwelcome place for the living to visit under any circumstances!

# Hanover

Most famous for its Hollenberg Pony Express Station State Historical Park Site; the original building is intact, restored, and still standing. There is an information center near the site for visitors.

The Hollenberg Pony Express Station was a way station for travelers going west, usually to California, Oregon, and Washington. Some were traveling to Arizona and New Mexico. Great and Sophia Hollenberg established this way station in 1857.

There are stories of residual and intelligent hauntings at the site and surrounding area. Shadow figures have been seen near the building. There have been reports over the years of voices and laughter heard in the way station, but no physical forms are attached to the voices and laughter! Visitors to the Hollenberg Pony Express Station will find it interesting in more ways than one!

The history surrounding most pony express stations and way or layover stations in general makes for enjoyable reading and research. As a mail route for the pony express, many of these sites were a most welcome place to reach after long trips from different parts of the country. In addition to the many ghost stories of horseback riders on their way to elsewhere, there are also the ghost stories of pioneers traveling through who may have fell ill and died at the stations or not far from the stations. Many a fine ghost tale is to be found concerning pony express stations throughout the United States, and each one carries its own peculiar paranormal occurrences.

If you can locate a historical route map of the numerous sites, you might find it interesting to visit their remains, as a good portion of them can still be located alongside modern highways. A collapsed way station alongside a major highway may cause pause to the driver who might wonder why such a thing stands alone and forlorn off the shoulder. If possible, stop and take a look. You might be surprised what you encounter at what was once a lively resting place alongside what has now become a forgotten ghostly route where only ghosts talk and laugh together! Touch a piece of the weathered, hardened wood from the frail ruins and close your eyes, and perhaps, just perhaps, in that fleeting moment you will have a ghost tell you his or her name and speak to you. Stranger things have happened.

# Hays

An army post, Fort Hays, is located in Hays, Kansas. Long known as a haunted location, the fort retains some of its military ghosts, which appear from time to time. However, of primary interest to ghost hunters is the legend concerning the ghost of Elizabeth Polly, who was living at the fort when a cholera epidemic broke out. Elizabeth became a heroine with her efforts to help the afflicted, but was felled by cholera and died in 1867. Her ghost is said to be dressed in blue and she sometimes wears a bonnet. Elizabeth has earned the name "The Blue Light Lady" and her ghost is oftentimes seen near Sentinel Hill, where her body is buried and marked by a monument to her.

Hays, Kansas, is located at the junction of Interstate 70 and Highway 183. As a personal note, let me share a paranormal experience that happened to me when I was at Hays, Kansas. An account of this encounter appears in further detail in the book, *Encyclopedia of Haunted Places* by Jeff Belanger.

The paranormal encounter took place on Old Highway 40, not far from Hays. It was late afternoon and I pulled off onto the shoulder of the highway because I had been driving for a long while and needed to rest. It was a nice day, pleasant and clear, and I fell asleep. I awoke to the sound of voices. Across from the driver's side of the car, where I had been sleeping, I looked out and saw a four-wheeled surrey with a fringe on its top; it was a two-seated, four-wheeled carriage with a dark brown top. I looked at the couple sitting in the carriage and they looked at me. The man reminded me of the late actor William Holden. The woman sitting beside him was young and pretty with dark hair. I would say their style of dress was typical of the clothes worn during the 1890s. I believe they were in their mid-thirties, age-wise. I waved to them and they waved back. I rolled the car window down to speak with them and that is when they slowly faded away and vanished from sight...

What I believe happened to me has happened to other people in such an instance — an encounter with a time vortex. People, under the right circumstances, can — *and do* —encounter time vortex settings. As I must have appeared a ghostly encounter to them in their time period, they, too, appeared as a ghostly encounter to me in my time period.

I have had other such encounters over the years in different places. It is possible someday I might encounter a particular time vortex that appeals to me, and I will step into it and then become another unexplained disappearance on the ghost roads of time! It is something for everybody to consider...as it can happen when you least expect it!

# Atchison

Considered to be one of the most haunted cities in the state of Kansas, Atchison is located on bluffs along the Missouri River in Northeast Kansas. The city has a special charm all its own, and its beautiful Victorian homes add further appeal to the city's setting. Much has been written about the paranormal happenings in this city, and programs on television have appeared about its ghostly background, including the "Haunted Town" episode on the Travel Channel.

## *Haunted Homes*

The city has numerous hauntings, and one of them is Atchison Street where accounts of shadow figures abound, voices calling to the living, and sightings of ghosts. In recent years, this street has come under more paranormal investigation due to its many hauntings, though many other streets also have their share of haunted homes.

### The Waggener Home

Also known as the Gargoyle Home, this house was built in 1885 by lawyer B. P. Waggener and is located at 819 North 4th Street. This Victorian home is one of the most haunted structures in Atchison.

The presence of ghosts has been documented by paranormal investigators and revolves around a reputed evil curse involving a pact Waggener made with the devil. This curse is considered by many to be still in effect and very much active. Many strange happenings, including the death of one of the house owners, have been attributed to this curse. Strange, flickering shadow figures have been seen around the house during the night and a strange wind is said to whisper through the top floor of the home and its roof. Many stories of ghosts being seen in and around the house have come down through the years since it was originally built and inhabited by B. P. Waggener!

### The Muchnic House

Constructed in 1885, there are various reports of a housemaid who fell down the steps and died there, and how she continues to make her presence known at different times.

Now an art gallery, the house is located at 704 North 4th Street. It was placed on the National Register of Historic Places July 12, 1974.

### Sallie's House

An unusual story of haunted "Sallie's House," located on North 2nd Street, concerns the death of a six-year-old child named Sallie. She was undergoing surgery by a doctor for appendicitis and died in the house before the surgery was completed. Her ghost is said to haunt the house at the location where she died. Sallie is affectionately referred to as "The Heartland Ghost."

Also, there is a story about an adult female ghost that haunts the house and the grounds. The appearance of a male ghost is sometimes seen walking the grounds during early evening.

## *Other Atchison Hauntings*

### Santa Fe Depot

This is a place where ghosts have been seen and heard. Built in 1880, there is the story of a man nicknamed Hangman Bill who fell and was killed in a train accident; his ghost is said to haunt the depot on an ongoing basis! Voices, footsteps, and shadow figures are oftentimes seen, and the ghost laughter of young women is heard west of the immediate area during the summer months. Stories of being touched by something have also been reported, although the ghost or ghosts reaching out to touch humans have not been seen.

Railroads, depots, and trains have always played an important role in hauntings, and the appearance of ghosts is common around such areas. It is as if during the passage of time, these places hang on to the various impressions of ghosts. These ghost hauntings can be residual and they can be intelligent. A residual haunting is one that is like a loop on a recording — it repeats itself and there is no contact between the ghost and the human. An intelligent haunting is one where the ghost is trying to make a connection or direct contact with a human.

Never underestimate the power of a railroad setting for having a bevy of ghostly inhabitants because, like haunted churches and other structures, impressions build up and grow stronger with the passage of time. This explains why railroad settings and churches, or areas where they once stood, can contain ghosts and paranormal activity when there appears to be no overt or immediate connection! I have found over time that there are places where a forgotten structure once stood but is no more, yet paranormal incidents are seen or documented at those places. A ghost may be dead, but that does not mean it is gone!

### The Missouri River

Over the decades there have been ghost sightings of bodies in the Missouri River near the city. On closer examination these ghostly presences vanish upon approach or simply disappear beneath the water's surface. Stories of floating heads and bodies are prevalent in ghost writings and documentations, and the reason is that there have been many drownings, murders, and deadly accidents in and around water since the dawn of history.

# Fort Leavenworth

This fort has a documented history of paranormal activity, hauntings, and ghosts dating back to when it was built in 1827. An active military prison with its own hospital, its stories of civilian and military ghosts are legendary. It is one of the longest running forts in American history and carries with it a wide selection of paranormal activity.

## *The Ghosts*

† General George Armstrong Custer is one of its most famous ghosts; his presence is seen often.

† Catherine Stutter, carrying a lantern and searching in a cemetery for her lost children, is another famous ghost whose presence has been seen.

† The ghost of Nez Perce Chief Joseph has been seen standing at different locations.

† Father Fred was killed in a fire. Now his ghost is seen dressed in his clerical clothing of the day and has even been photographed.

† The Lady in Black, thought to be the ghost of a nanny, communicates with young children.

† There is also the well-known story of fourteen German World War II prisoners of war hanged in an elevator in the prison hospital at Building 65 who scream out their pain and outrage frequently to those who can see and hear them!

† A soldier's suicide resulted in the sighting of a ghost at the Number 8 Tower, and the Officer's Quarters are also said to be haunted by past residents.

† The feeling of being touched has been reported often at various sites of the old fort, and the cemetery is alive with numerous ghosts.

~~~~~

There is indeed a strong mixture of both residual and intelligent hauntings on these ghostly grounds. Reports of being touched by ghosts at Fort Leavenworth are not uncommon, and shadow figures are also in abundance here.

# NEOSHO FALLS

A well-known and documented ghost town, Neosho Falls, Kansas, is located in Woodson County. A destructive flood destroyed the town in 1951, and shortly thereafter it became a deserted ghost town. Ruins of the town exist, as does its cemetery. If you're curious about investigating a haunted ghost town, this may be a perfect place for you to visit. Due to the condition of the ruins, it is best to be careful where you look.

There are stories of shadow figures in the cemetery and ghosts that walk what was once the town's main street. The ghost of a bearded elderly man in bib coveralls is reputed to walk the area and can be seen outside of different buildings; he appears to be searching for something or somebody. Upon approach, he vanishes and there is no trace of any footprints.

There is also the ruins of an old tavern that is, reputedly, haunted and is interesting to visit, view, and photograph.

Please let me say this: When you visit a deserted ghost town, whatever its condition, do respect its past and be careful to leave things intact as you come upon them. At one time, a ghost town was a thriving entity filled with people going about their daily business, but has now become obsolete and the human touch gone away. Still, any deserted town does have its ghosts — that is why it is called a *ghost town* — so respect the ghosts that live there and don't tear up what is left of their playground. Too many ghost towns have been carted away by visitors and souvenir hunters, and far too many ghost towns have been destroyed by vandals.

Also, remember that what items you might find in a ghost town and take home with you may be haunted themselves!

# LAWRENCE

This area that contains many ghost stories and situations involving paranormal activity. There is also a history of UFO sightings since the early 1960s.

## The Eldridge Hotel

Haunted by previous occupants, there are stories involving a woman in white, an elderly couple, a young man who killed his lover in one of the rooms, and a young woman dressed in 1950s attire looking for her father.

In addition, for the past twenty years there have been reports of some type of portal that opens at various times, although there is no documented record of any person disappearing into the portal wherever and whenever it does happen to appear.

## Lawrence Community Theater

Three ghosts — one male and two female — are said to haunt this theater. They were performers there when they were alive. When the theater is empty, employees working late will oftentimes hear running footsteps.

As a point of interest, old theaters are notorious for having paranormal activity. The older the theater, the more the activity and better the chance for the appearance of ghosts! I have been in theaters where I have seen residual hauntings and heard voices.

I think theaters tend to attract ghosts because a theater is generally a place where a play or movie is presented and the intensity of the emotions aroused can remain intact over time, given the right circumstances. In a way, it is like a snapshot of a scene from a slice of time that remains, settled into place, and enduring long after the actual occurrence! Theaters often house intelligent hauntings. The ideal situation is to be with a paranormal investigative team and capture the occurrence on film.

## *Haunted Universities*

### Haskell Indian Nations University

This university — and its Bell Tower — are settings for paranormal activity involving shadow figures, American Indian ghosts, uncanny sounds, and strange whispers. There is also a small cemetery containing Indian children who died an untimely death and it is said that the voices of these Indian children cry out for help to those who will listen.

The Bell Tower has unusual voices in the wind surrounding its base and structure; they can be heard at any given time. The university's Hiawatha Hall is another hotspot for macabre incidents.

Given the age and establishment of this university setting, it probably has both residual and intelligent hauntings. To examine the oftentimes cruel and unusual treatment of Native Americans in the United States is to see what the United States did to the nation's original settlers who inhabited the land before the onslaught of Europeans. The past history of Haskell Indian Nations University is the key to many of its current hauntings and paranormal activity, and it continues to be a setting for supernatural investigations.

### Wichita State University

Wichita State University is located in the city of Wichita, Kansas. It was originally named Fairmount College and was founded in 1886 by Rev. Joseph Homer Parker. The paranormal activity said to occur at this university includes ghost sightings of a residual nature.

### The University of Kansas at Lawrence

Founded in 1865 by the Kansas legislature, the university sits on top of a hill named Mount Oread in Lawrence, Kansas.

There is a story about an elderly, German-speaking man who haunts the Kenneth Spencer Research Library during the early afternoon hours. Upon approach, the ghost fades and disappears.

The Sigma Nu Fraternity is, reputedly, haunted by a woman who committed suicide inside the fraternity house.

# Chapter Two:
# MICHIGAN

With the nicknames of, among others, "The Lady of the Lake" and "The Great Lakes State," it's not surprising that the name of the state of Michigan means "Large Lake." Lansing is its capitol, though Detroit is the largest city.

The history of Michigan starts in the seventeenth century when it was first explored by the French; French settlers founded Saint Ignance in 1671. Admission to the Union came on January 26, 1837, when it became the twenty-sixth state. The birth of the automobile industry occurred in Michigan with Henry Ford's first auto plant. The Porcupine Mountains and Great Lakes add to the state's enduring charm as a setting for nature and the great outdoors.

Many famous people are connected with the state of Michigan, including Max Gail, Madonna, Lee Majors, Angela Jia Kim, Stacy Haiduk, James Earl Jones, Gillian Anderson, Nelson Algren, Michael Moore, Lily Tomlin, George Armstrong Custer, Jessica Rickert, Ty Cobb, Henry Ford, Gilda Radner, Terry O'Quinn, Grace lee Boggs, Joe Louis, Diana Ross, George Peppard, Sugar Ray Robinson, Gerald R. Ford, Tim Allen, Kay Givens McGowan, Francis Ford Coppola, Alice Cooper, Tom Selleck, Ruth Ellis, Robert Wagner, Nancy Kovak, Julie Krone, Betty Hutton, Julie Harris, and Edna Ferber.

## YPSILANTI

Paranormal hauntings in Ypsilanti revolve around ghosts of women brutally murdered there between 1967 and 1969. Known as the "Michigan Murders," the ghosts are frequently seen throughout the city.

St. Joseph Mercy Hospital is home to shadow figures and the ghosts of two elderly women patients who died there.

# BRIGHTON

The ghosts in Brighton, Michigan, are directly connected to the history of the Women's Correctional Institute. Not only were many prisoners executed here over the years, but also many prisoners were murdered, making it a place for paranormal occurrences. These are ghosts that, reportedly, make living persons around them feel a paranormal unease!

There are rumors of sexual crimes of long ago taking place that have lingered over the decades and disturb the living who encounter such things. Another aspect is said to be the unusual number of ghostly hitchhikers within two miles of the location. Some ghost sightings may be residual hauntings, but there is also the strong possibility that some intelligent hauntings are taking place.

Prison systems are rife with tales of hauntings and paranormal situations, and they generally carry with them a collection of sexual abuse occurrences. Many of these abuses involve rapes, sexual beatings, markings made by cutting, and various forms of castration and mutilation. Sexual mutilations are not uncommon practices in prisons, and much has been written about such cruel and degrading measures carried out by inmates against other inmates as an ongoing or permanent form of dominance control.

Such acts reflect a personal agenda and are usually well-planned before being done, and generally the perpetrator(s) go unpunished or are not identified. It has been documented that women prisoners who carried out such acts against other women prisoners are often more vicious than their male counterparts. The abuse is not limited to the United States, but found on a worldwide basis and easily found on the Internet and various media archives that contain pertinent information.

These books were suggested to me for research over the years, and now I pass this list on to those who might be interested: *Women Behind Bars* by Silja J. A. Talvi; *Prison Writings: My Life is My Sun Dance* by Leonard Peltier; *Prison Sexual Violence* by Daniel Lockwood; *Terror in the Prisons* by Carl Weiss and David Friar; and *Men Behind Bars* by Wayne Wooden and Jay Packer. Each book will shock and inform you, and make you angry that such things as prison abuse continue unabated in the twenty-first century.

# EAST LANSING

One of the most haunted university settings in the state is located in East Lansing. Michigan State University does not lack in paranormal occurrences or hauntings. To say the entire campus is haunted is to put it mildly, for everywhere on the campus is said to be some type of paranormal activity. Many areas are haunted, including Williams Hall, Mason Hall, Hubbard Hall, Mayo Hall, and Holmes Hall.

The ghosts of those who died on campus are reputed to be most active, and there are numerous accounts of shadow figures. The shadow figure is a permanent fixture on this campus. Sounds of strange laughter have been reported. Running footsteps are heard in different areas, but nobody has seen who makes them! Screams have been heard. This is a fine and respected institution of higher learning, despite its ghostly activities and things that go bump in the night or day.

# DETROIT

Built in 1912, the Detroit Masonic Temple is located in Detroit. Its builder, George D. Mason, who committed suicide there, haunts the building. In addition to the haunting by the ghost of George D. Mason, there are many shadow figures who appear and vanish at different times, the sound of a man crying, and a hazy discussion between two men about finances where the short conversation is unclear except for the words, "money came too late." The building has a reputation for having a macabre atmosphere that is at times stifling and uncomfortable accompanied by strange eerie noises in different rooms. The building has an abundance of orbs at night.

Grace Hospital, built in 1888, was a center of hauntings in its original time, but was demolished and replaced in 1978 to become the Sinai-Grace Hospital. One particular ongoing haunting was the known paranormal occurrence surrounding Room 401 on Corridor D of what was named the John R. Wing. This is where the legendary escape artist Harry Houdini died October 31, 1926. Over the years, visitors have told many stories of seeing the ghost of Harry Houdini walking corridors or watching people while leaning against the walls of the hospital. The hospital became part of the Detroit Medical Center in 1985. Many ghost hunters believe the hospital is haunted by its previous ghosts since it was rebuilt and consolidated on haunted grounds, and the abundance of ghosts still linger at the site.

# ANN ARBOR

A haunted mental hospital named Mercywood was once located on Jackson Avenue in Ann Arbor, Michigan. At one time, there was a small convent near the hospital where Catholic nuns lived and who worked at the hospital providing services and care for the patients. This old hospital was located not far from a cemetery. Although it has been torn down and the basement filled in, strange things are still occurring there. Another structure has been built on the site area since the hospital was condemned and destroyed.

Numerous stories and legends surround Mercywood Hospital and the cemetery near it. There are stories about the hospital basement, now filled in and under tons of dirt, which contains the wandering confused souls of many of the mental patients who died and whose frightened souls took refuge in that horrible basement amongst the belongings and trapped spirits of other inmates!

There are ghost stories of the inmates roaming the halls of the hospital during its years of operation, and even now, stories of shadow figures that lurk in the area and vanish into the ground are seen and reported. During its heyday, many reputed hauntings were said to have taken place in the rooms and basement of the hospital; there is also an undocumented tale of two inmates who killed each other — their ghosts are still seen in a death struggle during the summer months of the year.

With the passage of time, nobody recalls what was left in the basement and buried, nor was there any documents surviving that detailed the contents buried in the basement. It is said by those who live in the area that there is a distinct, defined feeling of creepy unease and discomfort for anybody who lingers too long in the area where Mercywood Hospital once stood. The cemetery not far from the hospital's original site is said to be haunted by orbs, shadow figures, and unseen things that reach out and touch the living who venture onto its burial grounds.

Mental hospitals are more apt to contain both residual and intelligent hauntings, even once the structure is vacant and abandoned or even demolished. These hauntings tend to be of an unsettling nature to the living that comes across them. This is due in part to many of the patients who suffered terrible mental anguish and mental disease. For many who died in such settings, they do not know they are dead, and their spirits still roam in the specific time dimension of that time in which they were patients in such institutions. There is a wide selection of such hauntings in paranormal literature; readers will find these hauntings and paranormal occurrences highly interesting — *but morbid* — reading.

Of the many theories concerning people who die in a mental hospital, three are more dominant than the others. The first theory is that the person dies and is free and passes over to the other side to find solace and peace. The second theory is that the person does not realize or recognize being dead and is doomed to remain between worlds until some action sets him or her free, if it ever does. Yet a third theory is that the person dies and is held in check between the world of the living and the world of the dead and is unable to escape this torment until he or she can complete some act or deed as a personal penance.

Mercywood Hospital is an incredible, *un-researched* setting from the past that continues to influence the present setting where it once existed. Perhaps some day various paranormal investigation groups will pool their resources together and reveal the hospital's dark secrets. It would be interesting to see what they come up with in their findings, and it would be intriguing what paranormal discoveries are revealed. At the time of its closing, it was a well-known mental hospital with an unusual history and record of events.

One grim legend has it that some of the bricks and timber from Mercywood Hospital was salvaged and used in building other structures throughout Ann Arbor. One has to pause and wonder what ghostly memories were imbedded in those bricks and timber used once more! Such paranormal occurrences can repeat themselves, as residual hauntings, if those imbedded memories survived.

To touch truly haunted objects is to feel their intensity, and in many cases, sense their unease, fear, and sense of dread depending upon what the original circumstances were. Examples of this are reactions received by touching a murder weapon, or possessing a souvenir from a Nazi Concentration Camp. For the potential paranormal collector at an undocumented and forgotten site, be wary of what you cart away as a personal souvenir, because you may well indeed be carting away something haunted you would not ever want in your personal life! Be careful in your paranormal investigations is a primary rule.

# MONROE

Active ghosts have inhabited the Monroe, Michigan, area since 1813. Historically, it is a battlefield setting and is remembered as the Battle and Massacre of River Raisin during the War of 1812.

One of the biggest battles fought was on January 22, 1813: three hundred American troops were killed during a hard-fought battle between the Americans and the British, aided by the Wyandot Indian Tribe led by Chief Roundhead. A detailed account of the military engagements can be found in various archival systems and on the Internet history sites. That the battlefield sites are haunted has been proven.

Recordings of ghost voices, orbs of different colors, and ghosts seen dressed in 1813 military clothes and clothes of that era have been witnessed during the day and at night. A hotbed for military ghost and battlefield activities involving ghosts, this area is continuing to prove valuable as a war setting for observing ghosts. There have also been sighting of women near the battlefield, and the ghosts of these women may have come looking for wounded loved ones or husbands. With the passage of time, it is becoming increasing evident that the immediate area of the city of Monroe, Michigan may have its share of ghostly occurrences and paranormal situations.

A good rule to keep in mind when investigating battlefield ghosts and related phenomena is to remember where there is one ghost there are many more just waiting to be discovered! Monroe, Michigan has more ghosts waiting in the wings, patiently waiting!

# BATTLE CREEK

Penfield Cemetery, located in Battle Creek, Michigan, is a cemetery with mysterious happenings. The paranormal activity includes:

† A trio of young girl ghosts are seen playing together with a large ball at the center of the cemetery.

† The ghost of an elderly man from the 1930s era walking in late afternoon at the cemetery and vanishes upon being approach by the living.

† A young man has been seen viewing grave markers at different places in the cemetery, but disappears upon being approached.

† There is also a story about an elderly lady who seems aware of being watched by the living, and upon approach, waves and smiles sweetly before fading into a light mist, and then she is gone.

† Orbs have been seen at early evening.

# BIRMINGHAM

Built in 1920, the Adams House is located in Birmingham, Michigan. There have been many documented paranormal happenings in this house, and the appearance of ghosts is prevalent.

Both female and male ghosts have made their presence known over the years and unusual sounds, including talking and whistling, have been heard. Many of these ghostly apparitions may be intelligent hauntings. Witnesses say that the house seems to attract paranormal activity and ghosts on an ongoing basis. Accounts of being touched by a ghostly presence have occurred — *and continue to occur* — in this house. There was even an incident where a female ghost, reputedly, groped a young man.

# DEARBORN

Well-known locally and internationally for its various ghostly encounters and paranormal occurrences, among the many haunted places in Dearborn, Michigan, are the Ritz Carlton Hotel, Greenfield Village, and the Henry Ford Museum.

The Ritz Carlton Hotel continues to be known as a place where male and female ghosts walk about. At this time, no photo documentation of these hotel ghosts is available.

Another haunted location is the Ford Rive Rouge Complex, nicknamed The Rouge. Since 1928, it has been one of the largest factories in existence anywhere in the world, and is considered one of the Ford Motor Company's finest auto production plants. Hauntings by deceased Ford employees are common.

# PETOSKEY

The ghost of Ernest Hemingway fishes on Walloon Lake here in Petoskey. This setting is believed to be the actual physical location for Hemingway's Nick Adams stories. These stories are about a young man's adventures in the great outdoors. The Hemingway family owned a summer home on Walloon Lake named Windemere near to Petoskey, and it is here that Hemingway spent his childhood learning to fish, hunt, and camp in the outdoors. This may have greatly influenced the stoic nature of Hemingway that comes across in his writings. The adventures he had as a childhood and teenager in this rugged Northern Michigan area firmly shaped his life outlook on the great outdoors and his ongoing love for outdoors adventure.

Hemingway's ghost is said to resemble the writer as he looked in the last years of his life, and there are stories of coming across the ghost fishing from the side of his canoe; other stories suggest a small wood boat. As an approach is made to the boat and its ghostly occupant, the small boat appears to move away from human contact, moving further away until it is gone. The Hemingway ghost never moves from its solitary position in the boat, nor does it ever look in the direction from which people have tried to hail it or attract it by calling out the name of Ernest Hemingway. Some stories suggest the Hemingway ghost laughs loudly and waves at those who have discovered him, and then the ghost boat and its ghost fisherman disappear together! There is a chance this could be a genuine intelligent haunting by the adult ghost of Ernest Hemingway, or it could be some type of residual haunting involving a time portal.

If a time portal is involved, then there are many things to consider. Depending upon who is doing the viewing, a time portal can involve *both* intelligent and residual hauntings. That time portals do exist, appear, and vanish, has been witnessed throughout recorded history. There are some paranormal and ghost investigators who believe that it's possible to step into a time portal and vanish with it when it closes. This would mean the person may remain there forever or, perhaps, some day return again to either the same instant of disappearance or many years further in time. Or, that person could reappear further back in time than when he or she originally disappeared!

I believe that time portals do exist and possibly could offer a logical explanation to some disappearances of people over the years. I do not believe that time portals can suddenly appear and swallow up a person. I believe a person has to willingly step into a time portal, or be coaxed to step inside one by some force or thing waiting on the other side. What the attraction would be to induce a person to step into a time portal would be known only to that person stepping into the time portal! Time portals and the paranormal seem interwoven.

Also, there is the strong suggestion made by some paranormal researchers that time portals are controlled by extraterrestrials and somehow involve UFO activity. There are various theories suggesting how time portals may occur and operate.

## Chapter Three:
# MINNESOTA

With many historic bridges and forts, Minnesota's natural beauty makes it one of the top states for outdoor sports, fishing, and hunting. Known as the land of 10,000 lakes, it actually contains 11,842 lakes and some of the oldest rocks on earth. As a geological area, it has a complex and involved history.

At a height of 2,301 feet, the state's highest point is Eagle Mountain. Original inhabitants were the American Indian tribes known as the Anishinaabe, Dakota, and Ojibwe. Saint Paul is the busy capital.

There are many famous people connected with the state of Minnesota, including F. Scott Fitzgerald, Tami Hoag, Carol Bly, Nob Dylan, Prince, Jim Arness, Peter Graves, Joel and Ethan Coen, Al Franken, Lea Thompson, Louis Erdrich, Sinclair Lewis, Garrison Keillor, Max Shulman, Judy Garland, Andrews Sisters, Kate Millet, Joan Drury, Patricia Wrede, Anne Tyler, and LaVyrle Spencer.

## WINONA

Winona State College was established here in 1858, and paranormal occurrences have been part of the site since the late 1800s. Its name was officially changed to Winona State University in 1975. The ghosts of deceased university presidents, John Ogden and William F. Phelps, haunt the campus.

## PIPESTONE

The Pipestone National Monument is located in Pipestone, Minnesota; it's where pipestone (catlinite) is dug from quarry sites to make Native American ceremonial pipes. These pipes are used

in American Indian religious and spiritual practices and use of the quarry areas dates back into the 1600s. During the early 1700s the Sioux tribes took possession of it. There is a visitor center near the quarry's location that contains an exhibit on petroglyphs. Daniel Sweet and Charles Bennett founded the town in 1876, and the Calumet Inn, built with quartzite in 1888, still functions as a hotel.

Ghosts of American Indians haunt Pipestone. It is reputed that these ghosts have been seen in the town and at the quarry sites. One

tall American Indian woman ghost was seen at the visitor's center and vanished upon approach.

The Calumet Inn is a remarkable stone structure and its hotel floors hold fifty functioning rooms for visitors to stay in. There are pleasant ghost stories of children playing in the halls, and couples from different eras seen walking in the halls. Whether these ghostly encounters and paranormal occurrences may contain some intelligent hauntings remains to be documented.

Another haunted location is the Pipestone County Museum, an old three-story building that contains the ghosts of two men and one woman, each seen on different floors. Also, the basement is said to have whispers and voices talking.

An interesting town, Pipestone, Minnesota, is a pioneering location for wind energy conservation and wind energy products. If you're interested in a place with a lot of history and pleasant and curious ghosts, Pipestone would be ideal to visit on vacation or as a visit to the town — it has many stories to share!

## ANOKA

Settled in the 1840s, Anoka, Minnesota, became a city in 1878. In 1878, the Rum River Dam was built. Several organizations came into being during Anoka's formative years, including the Free Masons (1859), Knights of Pythias (1872), and the Methodist Episcopal Church and Universalist Church (1854).

Anoka has several listings on the National Register of Historic Places, and it is said that the following ones have had paranormal occurrences and hauntings: Jackson Hotel, the Anoka Post Office, Banfill Tavern, the Anoka-Champlin Mississippi River Bridge, and

Riverside Hotel. These hauntings are considered both intelligent and residual in nature.

Originally named First State Asylum for the Insane in 1900, the mental hospital name was later changed to Anoka State Hospital in early 1937. The hospital contained both female and male patients. There have been apparition sightings both in the hospital and outside on the hospital grounds. Being a large medical setting, the location is conducive to situations that would attract both intelligent and residual hauntings. According to some reports, the tunnels said to lie beneath the buildings also contain the ghosts of former mental patients, and these ghosts are trapped in time; some of the ghosts seem to seek human contact, but no documentation has been carried out to verify such accounts.

When looking at mental hospitals, it is important to analyze and review the types of treatment used for mental illness; some of these treatments in the old days were rather severe, crude, cruel, and harmful. In many cases, deaths of patients happened as a result of such treatments. From the time it opened, Anoka State Hospital collected a good share of ghosts who had lived and died within its walls.

# LOON LAKE

The front of Loon Lake Cemetery overlooks the lake, and there is a memorial marker for the original Loon Lake settlers. Loon Lake Cemetery has been vandalized and abandoned to time, and the lake shore area is reputed to be haunted by ghostly mists and muffled voices.

A haunted cemetery is located not far from the shore of Loon Lake, and it is easy enough to get directions to it. Over the years there have been reports of ghost activity in the cemetery.

Legend has it that one or more Witches were buried in the cemetery and can be seen at night walking and talking together. Another story has it that only one Witch is buried there, and this person does approach cemetery visitors in the early evening hours only to stop a safe distance from them and suddenly vanish. Orbs have been seen. Strange sounds have been heard in the area during the night and morning hours.

Shadow figures have been seen in and around this cemetery, and many stories about paranormal occurrences have been handed down over the years concerning the lovely Loon Lake area. There is also a ghost story about a young girl dressed in pink that is singing — she appears suddenly, and then disappears as quickly as she arrived!

## Watery Secrets

Lakes and large bodies of water near shore have a paranormal history all of their own over a period of time. This is because the water is deep and holds *many, many* secrets!

Secrets lay buried in the silt and mud of a lake bottom long after the deed or action that placed them there has been committed. The psychic memory of the occurrence is embedded in the scene indefinitely. This accounts for why many paranormal occurrences are experienced while near a shore area, or while boating or swimming in a large lake near the shore. While fishing or swimming, you may find yourself coming into contact with something more than you bargained more! Just as humans enjoy a walk along a deserted shoreline, so do ghosts. If a cemetery is near the area, or something took place in the area that decided to linger on, you can be sure you are not alone in your personal walk! Ghosts may accompany you.

A drowning or murder involving a lake setting or along its shore is generally a sure bet to contain some paranormal activity related to that incident. What you suddenly see while out on your walkabout may indeed be there, so take a second look to be sure and talk with it. There is not any set season or temperature level in which a person can witness or encounter a ghost or a paranormal situation. To each, it's his or her own. Some people do have an affinity for ghosts, and certain ghosts certainly have an affinity for some living people. Never take a paranormal situation for granted, but investigate it because it may have a special meaning just for you or those living friends you are with!

I have found that I do have an affinity for ghosts and I have found my encounters have always been different. Whether I am alone, or most often in the company of other ghost investigators, I find I can hone in on the presence of a ghost if it is in the immediate vicinity, and I let my intuition guide me to where it is located. Some areas are more haunted than others, to recall an old phrase, and that is a true statement; also, some areas are more openly haunted to those who are keenly perceptive to such paranormal energy.

We must be acutely aware of the location in which we are searching for paranormal activity and be on constant alert to any valid signs it is there before us. If such paranormal activity is there waiting for a visitor, it will make itself known in a way that works best for the entity, especially if it is an intelligent haunting.

You will know if you are not alone. Whether it's a residual or intelligent haunting, that defined paranormal situation and its ghost is there for a given reason. It is up to you to find out what that reason is, but some mysteries will remain just that — mysteries.

# Northfield

Founded in 1855, Northfield, Minnesota, is a town of hauntings. The famous Malt-O-Meal plant is located there. Ames Mill was the original site for the plant and ghosts of former employees who worked there reputedly haunt it.

Northfield is the site of the infamous bank robbery attempt by Jesse James, Cole Younger, and their outlaw gangs in 1876. It is said that ghosts of these outlaws have been seen to appear in the alleys of the town, inside older buildings, and the ghost of Cole Younger at the old bank building.

## *Haunted School Settings*

### St. Olaf College
Founded during 1874 and established under the guidance of Pastor Bernt Julius Muus, St. Olaf College was named after Olaf II, the patron saint of Norway.

The college is also a place of many hauntings. Kelsey Theater, Thorson Hall, and other areas have had reports of ghosts, strange voices without bodies, odd whistling sounds, and touches by unseen hands, as well as people from different eras of time making their presences known.

## Carleton College

Founded in 1866 as Northfield College, James Strong was the first president of Carleton and promoted its Congregation Church emphasis. A financial patron of the college was William Carleton, after whom the college was later named.

The college is reputed to have shadow figures. The ghost of James Strong is said to haunt the campus and walk among its students when classes are in session.

# DULUTH

There are many haunted hotspots in Duluth, Minnesota. Among them is Gleensheen Mansion located on Lake Superior and owned by the University of Minnesota at Duluth. The large, sprawling mansion contains thirty-eight rooms and was built in 1905. The mansion has its original furniture and also contains artwork by many well-known artists including Henri Harpignies and Henry Farrer. A movie, "You'll Like My Mother," was filmed at the mansion in 1972.

The mansion's third floor and attic are haunted, and the ghosts of Elizabeth Congdon and her personal nurse, Velma Pietila, haunt the second floor; both women were murdered in the house on June 27, 1977. There are many ghost stories about this mansion, including a story about a child with demon eyes who haunts the kitchen and is seen during weekdays but not on the weekends.

An interesting aspect of demon children is the frequency in which they have turned up over the centuries in various writings from different countries. Demon children are known through both intelligent and residual hauntings — and they can be scary to encounter! An acquaintance once told me of her encounter with three demon children at a Missouri location. Describing it as a residual haunting, she said they reminded her of the extraterrestrial children in the original British black & white film, "Village of the Damned" (1960), starring George Sanders, Barbara Shelley, and Martin Stephens. She was referring to the "eyes" of the children. I understand. Other ghost investigators have seen such demon children, and it always comes back to those strange eyes that really are not eyes yet they are eyes... however strange those eyes may appear!

Another colorful story is of a young man running nude around the house at the midnight hour on Halloween, and when he is approached, vanishes near the right corner of the mansion and is not seen again until the following year. Two ghost cats are said to patrol the grounds.

A middle-aged, attractive woman dressed in 1930s attire is seen at the entrance to the mansion; she appears to be waiting for somebody inside to open the door and let her in. This is possibly a residual haunting, but the image of the woman and the look of expectancy on her face suggest the possibility that this could also be an intelligent haunting. It is reputed that she turns to look at the humans watching her and then fades into a hazy nothingness and disappears. Is that a warm, gentle smile on her lovely face as her image fades, or is she moving into another dimension while leaving behind a knowing look? Is she returning to a time era more comfortable to her personal feelings and, if so, what ghostly realm does she return to...only to appear again to human presences?

There is much to encounter at the Gleensheen Mansion, and under the right situations and circumstances you will. Maybe you will be the one to be greeted next!

# COTTAGE GROVE

Settled in the 1840s, Cottage Grove, Minnesota, is considered a bedroom community to St. Paul. Actor Seann William Scott is from Cottage Grove; his movies include "Bulletproof Monk" (2002), "Rundown" (2003), and "Southland Tales" (2007). Cottage Grove has two haunted cemeteries.

## Atkinson Cemetery

Orbs of different colors have appeared in this cemetery, and two male ghosts who are seen walking the grounds. They disappear upon approach. There is also a ghost cat here.

## Cottage Grove Historical Cemetery

Noted for its white orbs, a story about a reoccurring orange orb in the eastern section of the cemetery has also been told — it appears stationary before disappearing.

The ghost of an elderly woman in a long white dress who appears to be weeping walks the cemetery grounds, oblivious to everything. A little girl ghost in a blue dress is seen skipping about, and an elderly man in 1880s era clothes is seen talking with a woman from the same era. Both ghosts seem happy to be in each other's company, and they do not seem disturbed by the presence of living visitors to this unusual Minnesota cemetery.

## Chapter Four:
# ILLINOIS

One of the most complex sociological settings in the United States, as a state, Illinois' history of social innovations and the arts place it in the top twenty states. Chicago is the largest city, and Aurora is the second largest city.

Illinois is greatly blessed with a broad range of economic diversity, and many social scientists have said Chicago is the epitome of a true microcosm of the United States. Exploration of Illinois started in the 1600s. Indigenous people have lived along the rivers and in the woods of Illinois for over 7,000 years.

In 1847, following the dedicated efforts of Dorothea L. Dix, Illinois became one of the first states to establish a working system of state supported treatments for mental illness and disabilities. Catholic and Protestants are the largest religious groups in the state, and is also the home to a growing population of Hindus and Jews.

Museums, cultural events, music, and sports add to the lifestyles of the residents, with Illinois being home to some of the best jazz music on the contemporary scene. Jazz artists include many well-known names in the state, including composer/singer Paulinho Garcia, composer/pianist Bradley Parker-Sparrow, and singer Joanie Pallatto. Chicago is the home of Chicagosound, which includes Southport Records and Northport Records.

There are many famous people connected with the state of Illinois, including Ernest Hemingway, Betty Friedan, Black Hawk, Abraham Lincoln, Ronald Reagan, Frances McDormand, Clayton Moore, Richard Wright, Marlee Matlin, Hugh Hefner, Kim Novak, Michelle Obama, Warren Zevon, Maria Shriver, Robin Williams, William Holden, Walt Disney, Jane Addams, Miles Davis, Hillary Rodham Clinton, Harrison Ford, Dorothy Hamill, John Malkovich, Joan Allen, Ray Bradbury, Raquel Welch, James Jones, Benny Goodman, Jack Benny, Edgar Rice Burroughs, Rock Hudson, Alison Krauss, Robert Bloch, L. Frank Baum, Philip Jose Farmer, Jean M. Auel, Saul Bellow, and Carl Sandburg.

# CHICAGO

Some of the strangest paranormal occurrences and hauntings are said to take place in Chicago, Illinois. One such place is a house on West Chestnut Street. Built in 1879, it is a house covered in crosses and is, appropriately enough, known as the House of Crosses. It is reputedly haunted by one of the house's deceased inhabitants.

The disaster known as The Great Chicago Fire lasted from October 8-10, 1871. Over three hundred people were killed in the fire that destroyed four square miles of Chicago. To this day, the exact origin of the fire remains a mystery although it is said the fire started on DeKoven Street near the O'Leary property. The ghosts of some of

those who died in the fire still circulate in the area, and usually these ghosts are seen as fire victims and show burn markings.

Like most of the Chicago area, the Great Chicago Fire has contributed its fair share of ghostly hauntings and paranormal occurrences in the area of the original fire destruction. Buildings rebuilt on the charred remains are said to contain hauntings of the dead who perished in the flames of that horrible fire. There has been much written about victims of such fires, and due to the frightening and horrifying nature of such a death, there is often the possibility that some fire victim hauntings are of the intelligent kind. Most certainly, some of those fire victim hauntings are also residual in nature. That this fire still continues to haunt the imagination and cultural history of Chicago is no surprise, and neither are the prevalent ghosts associated with this disaster!

There have been stories of lizard people seen along the Chicago shoreline. These lizard people are considered capable of assuming human form and are able to shape-shift when coming into contact with humans. Many consider the lizard people part of some intricate paranormal connection, whereas many others consider them a curious and unfriendly extraterrestrial. Their presence has become more prevalent in recent years. Yet, the logical appraisal of the situation suggests that in reality there are several extraterrestrial races currently on planet earth whose motives are unknown.

## Iconic Ghosts

### Frank Sinatra

The ghost of Frank Sinatra, one of the legendary singers, performers, and actors of the United States, is said to haunt the popular nightclubs of Chicago, and his physical appearance varies with the storytelling. He is usually seen on the arm of some attractive lady going into a nightclub, sometimes he is seen smiling at couples as they walk along the way to theaters or fine eating establishments, and oftentimes he is seen as a young Sinatra lost in thought leaning up against a wall in one of Chicago's many art museums.

Frank Sinatra certainly needs no introduction. Much can be found about him and his life on numerous Internet sites and in books at libraries and bookstores. He was also a composer and gifted artist, and a collection of Frank Sinatra's selected paintings was published in book form by Random House in 1991 under the title of *A Man and His Art: Frank Sinatra*. Of course, as many readers will recall, of his vast number of song hits, one of those hits was the highly popular "Chicago," recorded and released in 1957.

Frank Sinatra remains an enduring icon in American culture.

## John Dillinger

Biograph Theater is located in Lincoln Park on Lincoln Avenue and it is one of Chicago's attractions as where the American gangster John Dillinger was shot to death by the FBI on July 22, 1934.

Dillinger was betrayed by Anna Sage. A Romanian prostitute who owned a popular brothel in Chicago, her real name was Ana Cumpanas. She was nicknamed "The Woman in Red" for her role in trapping Dillinger. She died in 1947.

This is the scene of a popular haunting legend in which three scenes take place, depending on who is telling the story. One haunting has John Dillinger talking with Anna Sage in front of the theater; the second haunting has Dillinger appearing at the theater standing on the sidewalk; and the third haunting involves the famous shootout and killing of Dillinger near the alley of the theater. No photographic documentation of these hauntings has taken place despite the enduring legend of these ghostly apparitions!

Other John Dillinger haunting scenes have been reported in the Biograph Theater itself — he has been seen in the audience, in the lobby area, looking back at theater patrons through restroom mirrors, and standing in front of the door in the men's restroom.

With the passage of time, such haunting situations take on a life of their own and the ghosts become part of the cultural heritage of the American Gangster Era of the 1930s, with the telling oftentimes becoming more involved and dramatic! John Dillinger has been the focus of many books and movies since his death, including the 2009 film release, "Public Enemies," which starred Johnny Depp as John Dillinger, Christian Bale as FBI agent Melvin Purvis, and Stephen Lang as the FBI agent (Charles Winstead) who had shot Dillinger dead. A side note of interest: Melvin Purvis committed suicide in 1960 and there have been sightings of his ghost at the Biograph Theater.

## Bloody Mary

Of course, no look at the city of Chicago would be complete without mentioning the legendary tale of "Bloody Mary." She is said to come to whoever calls her, if that person stands before a mirror and calls out her name in a loud, strong voice three times. After saying her name three times, the caller waits. She may appear in the mirror in place of your face, and part of the ongoing legend is that you may ask her questions and she may answer them. Yet, on the other hand, you may suddenly find the person of Bloody Mary standing next to you and she is intent of killing you for disturbing her peace!

## Al Capone

Sightings of Chicago's most famous gangster, Alphonse Capone, have occurred in the many different locations he frequented in Chicago. A grisly setting Capone engineered was the St. Valentine's Day Massacre on February 14, 1929; this resulted in the murder of seven men against a brick wall in an old warehouse. For decades, it was said people could touch the wall of this murder scene and hear the screams of the dying men, or stand and study the wall and suddenly see the bodies of the men shot and falling lifeless to the ground. Other stories surfaced, but those were two of the many. Paranormal investigators suggest this is a residual haunting, and although the warehouse was destroyed during late 1967, there are still sporadic tales that sightings of the dying men are seen near the original site and elsewhere in the city.

# LEMONT

The Saint James Sag Catholic Church and cemetery is located in Lemont, Illinois. It was established in 1917 and is located near Archer Avenue. The cemetery is said to have orbs of various colors, and there are stories about the ghosts of chanting monks who roam the grounds and cemetery.

The ghosts of a woman with a small boy have been seen in the east side of the cemetery during the summer months. The church and cemetery also have shadow figures that appear at nightfall.

# BARTONVILLE

An insane asylum famous for the doctor who pioneered positive approaches to helping the mentally ill is located in Bartonville, Illinois. This immense hospital contains four cemeteries on the premises, and at one time in its mysterious history consisted of forty-seven buildings.

Built in 1895, the Peoria State Hospital was also known as Bartonville State Hospital for the Insane. During its apex in the late 1950s, it held nearly 3,000 patients. The hospital ceased operations and was permanently closed in 1973. As of this writing, the property is privately owned and no trespassing applies to the entire site.

Dr. George A. Zeller was in charge of the hospital in its formative years and pursued a humane approach of kindness and understanding toward the mentally ill in his charge, and he advocated tolerance in treating the mentally ill. He observed many mysterious paranormal occurrences at the hospital including the death and passage of the grounds gravedigger, Old Book, and the Graveyard Elm.

Zeller's remarks about the hospital were well-known and published in the media. Although I was unable to track down any of his writings, I found that he did write two books relevant to the ghostliness of the hospital. I do not know if these two books were privately printed or published in a limited run by a little known publisher. Should you come across either title, it would be most interesting to read and ponder over Dr. Zeller's recall of what took place at Peoria State Hospital. These two books are, with approximate publication dates, as follows: *The Bereft* (1926) and the autobiography *Befriending the Bereft* (1935); it is possible that there was only one book with the word "bereft" in the title. Zeller died in 1938. I did come across some references to a book, *Asylum Lights* by James S. Ward (2008?), which reprints some of Zeller's personal stories and material about the mental hospital. I would say that Zeller's stories about this mysterious hospital would be well worth your reading time if they can be located.

That the four cemeteries on site are haunted with both intelligent and residual hauntings is part of ongoing investigations by legitimate paranormal researchers. Again, the reader is cautioned that this large complex of medical buildings and its four cemeteries are on private posted property and not open to random explorations!

Further research will disclose that, unlike many such hospitals of its day, torture and cruel experimentation did not surface at Peoria State Hospital. It is a documented fact that such practices did exist to some degree and were actively pursued as cures at the Choate Mental Health Hospital and the Elgin State Mental Hospital. The ghosts of these two hospital settings are reputed to still haunt the actual sites where they suffered and were experimented upon. Zeller maintained a commitment in Peoria State Hospital that no such horrors would take place, and such things did not happen on his watch, and evidentially, he was much beloved by the patients, his staff, and his peers.

## HOMER GLEN

Home of the respected Vivekananda Vedanta Society of Chicago, which was founded at Chicago in 1930 by Swami Gnaneswarananda, this Ramakrishna Math is now situated at its new location on 14630 South Lemont Road, Homer Glen, Illinois. It is a well-known spiritual center.

There is a story that the ghost of a young Vedanta monk went to the new, larger facilities at Homer Glen from the old location. He is seen during the summer months walking in the vicinity.

## ALTON

Considered to be one of the most haunted cities in Illinois, one of Alton's most famous haunted locations is the Mineral Springs Hotel. Now named the Mineral Springs Mall, this hotel has seen its share of deaths, including murders and suicides. Some sightings in the rooms and basement include the presence of orbs — there are six rooms noted for an abundance of orbs. The ghost of a young girl wearing a white dress has been seen, and also the ghost an elderly lady seen staring out from a window. Voices have been heard in the basement and the restrooms. Many other ghost stories abound in this charming hotel.

The McPike Mansion, built in 1869, is said to have ghosts. These ghosts were inhabitants of the stately house over the decades, and they seem comfortable in remaining where they are! The mansion has sixteen rooms, a basement, and a wine cellar, and is in the process of undergoing renovation. Now privately owned, it is a favorite among seekers of the paranormal.

Another much haunted location is the Mansion House built in 1834. In 1864, it was used as a hospital to treat a smallpox epidemic and, as a result, there are numerous stories concerning apparitions at the Mansion House. Ghosts of Catholic nuns have been seen, as have ghosts dressed in the clothes of the 1860s era. Many ghosts from different time periods have been reported to haunt the Mansion House since its construction.

There are other hauntings and paranormal occurrences at Alton, and they are usually associated with some of the old business buildings and houses in the city. When there are an abundance of old structures with ongoing habitation, there is generally an abundance of ghosts. Paranormal occurrences can include whisperings, voice, the sounds of coughing or walking, and there is always the puzzling possibility of what is referred to as farting ghosts.

Farting ghosts are not seen, but they are often smelled, as they "perfume" the air with a rank odor. In my paranormal research and investigations, I have not, as of this writing, come into contact with a farting ghost; however, I have visited with people who have claimed such a dubious encounter, and the ghost went on its merry way, so to speak! Maybe you will have the distinction of encountering such an apparition during your ghost hunting!

# VISHNU SPRINGS

Named after the culturally respected and revered god of Ancient India, for a time Vishnu Springs was a popular health village known for its healing waters. The ruins of the Capitol Hotel are still intact, but nothing remains of this village once found in a charming valley along the Lamoine River in McDonough County.

Darius Hicks started the town of Vishnu Springs by selling land plots owned by his family. He reputedly haunts the Capitol Hotel, and other residents who lived in the area are said to now walk the valley in peace as ghosts.

In its early years, the town flourished, but with the passage of time the businesses closed and the town became abandoned. In 2003, the land was donated to Western Illinois University as a wildlife refuge.

# OAK PARK

Oak Park, Illinois, is known as the birthplace of American novelist Ernest Hemingway. He was born there July 21, 1899. Hemingway lived in a six-bedroom Victorian house and attended the Oak Park and River Forest High School from which he graduated high school. Hemingway's concise, terse style of writing has a positive, understated approach with its short sentences and strong narrative; his writing style has had a lasting influence on American literature, and influenced many authors. There has been so much written during Hemingway's life about him, as well as after his death, that a sizeable library could be built up simply by amassing the many books available on the writer. Some of his most important writings, which are today considered American literary masterpieces, and world favorites include *The Sun Also Rises* (1926), *A Farewell to Arms* (1927), *For Whom the Bell Tolls* (1940), *The Old Man and the Sea* (1952), *A Moveable Feast* (1964), *Islands in the Stream* (1970), *The Garden of Eden* (1986), and *The Complete Short Stories of Ernest Hemingway* (1987).

Hemingway was awarded the Pulitzer Prize for Fiction in 1953 and the Nobel Prize for Literature in 1954. He committed suicide at age 61 on July 2, 1961, at his home in Ketchum, Idaho. His writings continue to remain popular throughout the world. In addition, there are many unpublished writings that he left behind.

Over the years since Hemingway's death, there have been reported sightings of his ghost near the vicinity of his birth home during the summer months. He is seen as a husky man in his late thirties staring at the house for a short time, then briskly turning and walking away, fading into a soft mist then vanishing; reports say he is wearing summer clothes and his trademark moustache. Attempts to approach the Hemingway ghost have resulted in its immediate disappearance. There are numerous sightings of famous ghosts throughout the world. Ernest Hemingway is one of them. Hemingway's ghost has been seen in places he frequented, including his homes in Illinois, Cuba, and Idaho, and in the apartments and cafes he frequented during his active lifetime. It is not surprising.

# Chapter Five:

# Indiana

Indiana residents are known as Hoosiers, and the state's name means "Land of the Indians." The French explorers opened the area to trade and made ongoing trade agreements with the Native Americans in the region during the late 1600s and firmly established trade and trading posts by 1732.

Indiana played important roles in both the American Revolution and the American Civil War due to its strategic location. The Wabash River is one of its major waterways, and manufacturing is important to its economy. Indiana is a colorful state with a long colorful history, and much has been written about it over the years following World War II.

There are many famous people connected with the state of Indiana, including siblings Michael and Janet Jackson, Rex Stout, Forrest Tucker, Florence Henderson, Booth Tarkington, Cole Porter, Larry Bird, Anne Baxter, Ernest Pyle, Hoagy Carmichael, James Dean, Red Skelton, Twyla Tharp, Jessamyn West, Theodore Dreiser, and Scatman Crothers.

# Hymera

A place of known paranormal occurrences, Hymera, Indiana, was incorporated into a town in 1902, with settlers dating back into the 1800s. Remembered primarily as a mining town, there are several places reputed to be haunted, including Alum Cave and its immediate area with the ghosts of the miners who worked there.

The ghost of American Revolution War hero Nathan Hinkle haunts Hymera Cemetery, where orbs have been seen at his grave. A fifteen-foot monument marks his resting place.

Shadow figures and ghostly apparitions also frequent the cemetery, and there's a strong prevalence of colored orbs.

# Fairmont

Legendary actor James Dean is buried at Park Cemetery in Fairmont. Born at Marion, Indiana, February 8, 1931, Dean was killed in an unusual automobile accident in Cholame, California, September 30, 1955. Accompanied by his friend and mechanic, Rolf Wutherich, Dean was driving his recently purchased Porsche 550 Spyder when he and another driver hit head on. Although Wutherich survived his injuries, Dean did not.

James Dean was an icon for his generation, and much has been written about him. Many claimed he was a bisexual whose love affairs was the talk of Hollywood and that he planned to give up acting to become a movie director. He is also said to have had some interest in the occult and the philosophy of existentialism. His gravesite is said to be haunted.

Many people are said to have seen James Dean standing at his gravesite, silently looking down at where his body lays buried. There have also been reports of him speaking to those who approach his ghost; reputedly, he acknowledges being seen — and then he simply smiles and disappears from view.

James Dean has been a favorite topic for writers since his untimely death at age 24, and probably will continue to be so indefinitely. He made only three films, which remain as his enduring movie legacy: "Rebel Without a Cause," "East of Eden," and "Giant." Stories of ghost hauntings involving Dean have also been reported elsewhere. James Dean is a major historical icon of the 1950s decade and his popularity continues to this day.

# CHESTERON

Home of the Wizard of Oz Festival, there are many tourist attractions in this old city called Chesteron. Some of the cemeteries are reputedly haunted, and orbs have been seen in them during the early evening hours. Places known to have paranormal occurrences or hauntings include the Chesterton Historic District and Chesterton City Hall.

Though generally known to have ghosts, Chesterton is home to one of the most famous ghosts in the state. Her name was Alice Marble Gray and in real life — as in death — the lovely nude woman was seen in the Indiana Dunes, where she enjoyed nature freely and without interruption. It is said that after her death she returned to her beloved dunes and is seen to this day. It remains unclear whether or not her presence is an intelligent haunting. Some claim to have spoken to her ghost whereas others say she vanishes upon approach.

A rich archeological setting, the Indiana Dunes were settled as early as 14,000 years ago. The French first explored the area in the late 1660s.

# PERU

Founded in 1834 by William N. Hood, Peru, Indiana, is known as the Circus Capital of the World. The Miami Courthouse, as well as several of the city's very old buildings, is said to be haunted.

Cole Porter (1891–1964) was born in this city, and it is said that on clear nights he walks the sidewalks of the city and has been seen at his gravesite in Mount Hope Cemetery. This cemetery contains over 13,000 internments and is an old, well-kept, and attractive cemetery. The Cole Porter Festival is held annually here, and the Cole Porter Birthplace and Museum is part of the city's tourist attractions.

Cole Porter remains one of the United States' most important composers and lyricists; his music is beloved throughout the world. Among his many songs, considered Great American Standards, include "You Do Something To Me," "Anything Goes," "Night and Day," "True Love," "In The Still of the Night," and "I Concentrate On You." Ella Fitzgerald, Frank Sinatra, Tony Bennett, Johnny Mathis, and Judy Garland are considered by music critics as some of the important vocal interpreters of Porter's popular songs.

A version of Porter's life appeared in 1940 as the movie, "Night and Day," which starred Cary Grant as Porter and Alexis Smith as Linda. A more accurate account of his life, which included his homosexual encounters, appeared in the 2004 movie "De-Lovely" starring Kevin Kline as Porter and Ashley Judd as Linda. Cole Porter was married to Linda Lee Thomas for over thirty-four years until her death, at which time he became a recluse and no longer wrote music. During their long and devoted marriage, his wife Linda conceived and miscarried several times, much to Cole and Linda's sadness.

Cole Porter is buried next to his wife at Mount Hope Cemetery. It is rumored that cemetery visitors have seen the ghosts of Cole and Linda Porter walking and talking together. Cole Porter's grave is one of the most visited in the state of Indiana.

# INDIANAPOLIS

A modern city with a wide range of hauntings, Indianapolis is the largest city in the state of Indiana. Its strong economy is primarily based on manufacturing. The city became the state capitol in 1820 after the Native American tribes of the Delaware and Miami were successfully removed. Founded on the White River, this river is the main tributary to Wabash River.

## Crown Hill Cemetery

There are many haunted cemeteries in Indianapolis, with Crown Hill Cemetery one of its most haunted. Occupying 555 acres, the cemetery is ranked as the third largest cemetery in the United States with nearly 200,000 graves. Originally established in 1864 as Greenlawn Cemetery, and later renamed Strawberry Hill Cemetery, this burial area was located in a heavily wooded forest that gave rise to tales of strange sounds and mysterious happenings. At the heart of this area was a swamp inhabited by bears and other wild animals, but eventually it was converted to burial site usage. It is said that the Gothic Chapel and Peace Chapel at the cemetery have been scenes of paranormal occurrences.

Three ghostly hauntings concern the graves of Alexander Hannah, John Dillinger, and novelist Booth Tarkington; a popular American writer, Tarkington's many books gained him an international following of readers. They include *The Gentleman from Indiana* (1899), *Penrod* (1914), *The Magnificent Ambersons* (1918), *The Ghost Story* (1922), and *The Show Piece* (1947). On clear nights when the cemetery is quiet, there is said to be seen the ghosts of the three men at different parts of the cemetery walking about. The smiling ghost of Booth Tarkington has also been seen during the daytime not far from his resting place. *(Note: For the curious wanting to see where one of America's most notorious criminals is buried, you can locate John Dillinger's grave in Section 44, Lot 94.)*

Other stories of paranormal occurrences include the appearance of orbs, and the sounds of crying heard towards the south section. There are many residual hauntings in Crown Hill Cemetery, and the possibility of some intelligent hauntings is evident based upon the many stories told over the decades.

## *Central State Mental Hospital*

Originally a hospital setting for the insane, Central State was founded in 1848. It was known to contain a chapel that was haunted from its earliest days in existence. The hospital has a series of tunnels running beneath the buildings. Many horrible incidents took place here, and the torturing of inmates was not unusual in its early days. It was closed in 1994, but its paranormal occurrences and hauntings live on. One important aspect of the hauntings, which is often found at other such mental institutions of long standing, is the appearance of ghosts that appear and then vanish upon approach. There are bodies buried at the location; some burial sites are known and some are not. Various people have witnessed scenes of patients being robbed, some screaming and running in fear, over the years.

Central State Mental Hospital is a reputed lure to ghost hunters, and it is said that those seeking contact with ghosts and the paranormal may find more than they bargained for at this hospital. An area referred to as the old autopsy room building is a favorite site for ghost investigations — it is said to always provide something macabre on its premises! No doubt that this is a great place to go looking for ghosts. There are reports of intelligent hauntings and people being touched by the fingers of *visible* ghosts, but, as of this writing, no photographic documentation exists. The torturing, sterilizations, and beatings that took place in this setting are part of its enduring history of paranormal happenings and, as a result, Central State Mental Hospital is a place of ghosts, orbs, and lingering terrors from those who died there. One wonders, what were some of these deaths caused by?

## The Slippery Noodle

Built in 1850, Slippery Noodle is one of the state's longest running drinking establishments and remains one of the most unusual bars anywhere! The poet, James Whitcomb Riley, visited this bar during his lifetime, and it is said on lonely, quiet evenings when the moon is full, his ghost is seen having a drink in the bar. From its beginning, this inn underwent many name changes and many owners! The upstairs has small rooms, and the basement is reputed to have two bodies buried in it. John Dillinger was a known visitor to this bar.

An intelligent haunting situation involving a tall, muscular black man is said to happen often in the basement, as his ghost attempts communication with the living. Sounds of walking and laughter are heard, and shadow figures are seen during the day and at night. At one time the inn was the setting for a bordello and there is a story of a murder happening during the bordello's business hours. Bordello settings can offer unusual hauntings, many of which are unnerving. There is much to be discovered about this haunted inn located at 372 South Meridian Street, and its nearby cemetery. It is the stuff that paranormal occurrences and hauntings are made of!

# FRANKLIN

Established in the 1800s, Franklin, Indiana, is named after Benjamin Franklin. It is the home of Franklin College, which was founded in 1834; the college is said to have both hauntings and paranormal activity.

Not immune to hauntings, the city has an interesting history and was important during the American Civil War due to its location. An elderly woman who vanishes upon approach reportedly haunts the second floor of the Johnson County City Hall.

The old movie house, Artcraft Theater, opened in 1922 and closed in 2000 expect for special events. Known for its art deco architecture and designs, its concession stand and lobby rest upon an imaginative black and white checkered floor. There is the story of a young couple talking near the concession location, but, when spoken to, the couple disappears.

# BLOOMINGTON

Located in Bloomington is a cemetery that is one of the most talked about in the state for its paranormal activity and ghosts. The directions to this haunted place are easy to follow. It is located directly off of Old Highway 37 and connects to the Morgan-Monroe State Forest. There is a stone wall along the highway that pinpoints the entrance. Walking to this haunted cemetery, feelings of unease permeate its living visitors, and there is a sense of dread and deadly stillness in the cemetery where the bodies lay buried.

Ghost stories abound, and there is evidence to suggest some of these apparitions are intelligent hauntings. Different female ghosts have been reportedly seen; each are said to be dressed in clothes of their given eras and each has a different approach to those daring to command her attention. Some people report a feeling of the ground moving under their feet…as if something unseen beneath the soil wishes to swallow them and have them join the ranks of the dead!

Ghost animals have also been sighted at this cemetery, and visitors have mentioned an eerie moaning sound in the wind. There have also been reports of strange, unidentified lights in the sky above the cemetery… This is a very haunted cemetery, indeed!

# Chapter Six:

# Iowa

Despite a strong manufacturing base, Iowa has a diverse economy that has greatly helped the state to weather hard economic times. Like most Midwestern states it has a humid continental climate.

Iowa takes its name from the Ioway people, an early American Indian tribe living in the region during the time of European exploration. American Indians were in the state over 13,000 years ago, and one prehistoric tribe was the Oneota. Other tribes include the Dakota, Otoe, Ioway, Ho-Chunk, Sauk, Meskwaki, Omaha, and Illiniwek. The French opened the state to trade after 1673.

The removal of the Indian population started in 1814 and was completed in 1850. During the American Civil War, Iowa provided the most soldiers of any state — and took some of the heaviest casualties in the war. Iowa troops fought at the bloody Battle of Wilson Creek near Springfield, Missouri.

On April 3, 2009, the Iowa Supreme Court ruled in the Varnum vs. Brien case that same-sex marriages were legal. It was the first Midwest state to permit same-sex marriages.

Iowa has a wide range of sports and educational activities, and there are many famous people connected with the state. They include Taimah, Donna Reed, Aldo Leopold, Sara Paretsky, Quashguame, Glenn Miller, Andy Williams, Billy Sunday, Sullivan Brothers, Herbert Hoover, Peggy Whitson, Nile Kinnick, John Wayne, Grant Wood, Julie Adams, Mackinlay Kantor, Ann Landers, Jean Seberg, Keokuk, Marjorie Cameron, Bix Beiderbecke, Appanoose, Macdonald Carey, Cloris Leachman, and George Reeves.

# Davenport

Musician and jazz composer Bix Beiderbecke was born in Davenport, Iowa, March 10, 1903; now he reportedly haunts his birthplace, as witnesses have claimed seeing him there. Bix died at age 28 on August 6, 1931. His childhood home was at 1934 Grand Avenue.

Bix Beiderbecke became a legend in the years following his untimely death from alcoholism and pneumonia. He played cornet and piano and had a tremendous influence on jazz musicians including Louis Armstrong. Among his many recorded songs are found "Toddin' Blues," "Davenport Blues," and "Riverboat Shuffle."

Bix Beiderbecke is buried in his family's plot at Oakdale Cemetery. His ghostly presence has been reported at both his childhood home and his family burial site. When seen, the ghost appears lost in thought and at peace.

## BOONE

The site of where coal mining was started in 1849, the town of Boone, Iowa, was established in 1865. One of its tourist attractions is the Puffer-billy Day Festival.

This town is where the State Nursing Home and Hospital was located. Residual and intelligent hauntings have said to occur in this formidable medical setting, with some of the ghosts described as being *angry* ghosts. Like many such paranormal settings, there are different versions of different hauntings; occurrences include moans, crying, shouting, and being touched by things that hurriedly rush by the living!

What was once a standing structure is now only a vague memory to the living. Ruled hazardous, the building was condemned and eventually demolished in 2005. However, ghosts do not necessarily go away when the building they haunted goes away, as this case would indicate. The restless ghosts are, reportedly, still there doing as they have always done!

## WILLIAMSON

The mysterious Stoneking Cemetery can be found in Williamson, Iowa. This cemetery is reputed to have a long-standing curse upon it, and there have been many reports of paranormal activity on its grounds and in nearby areas. Heavily haunted by ghosts, it is also a haven for shadow figures that live there with the dead.

Strange moaning sounds have been heard, and also the wet sound of something described as the dying gurgle from a slit throat. Both intelligent and residual hauntings are said to occur there.

Stoneking Cemetery is a legend in the city, and is perhaps one that hides more secrets than yet known to those who explore its ghostly holdings!

# Council Bluffs

The Black Angel Statue, located in Council Bluffs, is, reportedly, the site of many paranormal occurrences. What mysterious secrets does the Black Angel Stature hold for the living? Its hauntings include:

† An elderly man with a cane is sometimes seen. If you get too close to him, he will look at you, raise his cane, whisper some words not clearly heard, frown, and then disappear.
† An elderly couple is sometimes seen staring at the Black Angel Statue. Upon approach, they simply vanish — as if stepping back into a portal that cloaks them.
† Visitors have reported being touched by something solid — *and invisible*.

# Muscatine

A huge, expansive bridge going over the Mississippi River that connects two land areas is located in Muscatine and ghosts of people from different eras have been seen walking it — ghosts that suddenly disappear as quickly as they appeared! At one time in its early history, the city was nicknamed "Pearl of the Mississippi" when pearl buttons were made from shells at the McKee Button Company.

The *Muscatine Journal* was the newspaper established in 1840. Founded in 1833 and later named Muscatine in 1849, one of the explanations for the city's unusual name was that it came from the Mascoutin Indians.

The Muscatine County Courthouse is a three-story structure said to be haunted. Although many structures may no longer exist, the ghosts do not know that and continue to make their appearances known to the living.

The Old Hershey Street Hospital was long known for its shadow figures and ghostly activity. Sounds of crying were heard, and some claim that *invisible* hands have touched them. The second floor also contained the ghost of a young boy in a hospital gown searching for his mother.

No longer in existence now, at one time the Old Story County Home was a known site of apparitions and paranormal happenings. The original Lutheran Homes, with its small cemetery, was also known for its hauntings involving ghosts of children. These children were most often seen in the cemetery. The original Hotel Muscatine was said to have ghosts in twenty of its rooms, and the ghost of a janitor who haunted the basement.

It is interesting to remember when investigating old hotels, court houses, or related structures, where many people came and went, that one of the first places to examine for hauntings is in the basement. Whether residual or intelligent hauntings, there is usually a good likelihood that a trip to the basement will turn up something!

In some cases, a trip to a restroom in these buildings may turn up more than a simple visit! Many restrooms are haunted, and there are many tales told of being in a toilet booth, or standing before a urinal, or standing at a sink, and having *something* reach out and touch you! Nothing could be more macabre in such a situation than to have something touch you and whisper in your ear at the same instant.

# Algona

An unusual cemetery is located in Algona, Iowa — it has gypsy ghosts! It is said this graveyard holds the spirits of many gypsy people who died near there.

Shadow figures have been seen and crying has been heard. A ghost dog has been seen wandering about — it vanishes when somebody calls out to it. Orbs have been seen during the night hours.

# Cedar Falls

The city of Cedar Falls has its own peculiar hauntings as well, and the city seems ripe for paranormal investigations. William Sturgis founded the city in 1845 and is said to be among the notable ghosts haunting it.

The city's eleven main cemeteries have reported hauntings, both residual and intelligent. The ghosts are previous inhabitants of the city's long history.

Orbs have been seen in the Little Red Schoolhouse, built in 1909 on the site of an older building. Other haunted areas needing more paranormal investigation include the Cedar Falls Ice House, Diamond Bros. General Store, and the Empress Theater.

## University of Northern Iowa

Cedar Falls, Iowa, is where the University of Northern Iowa and its haunted campus theater reside. Bartlett Hall is also known for being haunted by paranormal happenings.

This education complex was originally opened in 1869 and was known as Central Hall. It was named the University of Northern Iowa in 1967. In less than a hundred years, it had become one of the finest educational centers in Iowa, and is the publisher of *The North American Review*.

Certain areas on campus are more haunted than others. Bartlett Hall, Bender Hall, and the Strayer-Wood Theater have an ongoing history of paranormal occurrence and hauntings.

## Empress Theater

Opened in 1910, it had a short life as a silent theater, but over the decades it had a colorful existence. The theater has since been restored — ghosts of previous moviegoers reportedly haunt the restrooms!

An interesting aspect of old movie theaters is that many of them have haunted restrooms. Why? Because of the activity generated by people taking a short respite or to meet someone. I have been told over the years that more deals have been struck and agreements reached between consenting parties in movie theater restrooms than can be imagined! After all, the United States has always been in love with the movies and its actors and actresses. Look at the blockbuster releases today and it is little surprise that restrooms and lobby areas are more than just that — they have become a cultural setting for quick observations, fast visits, agreements of one kind or another, and places to make arrangements for future meetings. It is no surprise then, given the hectic pace of today's schedules and stress that we meet up with ghosts in such settings. We may not recognize them as ghosts at first, and then again, we might! They may be dressed slightly different, or they might not seem to be in sync with the surroundings, but they can bump into us in a psychic manner of one sort or another. They do leave their psychic impressions, and in the end, that is what ghosts really do best — leave impressions that are either residual or intelligent hauntings. Who could ask for anything more than such a chance meeting with a ghost in a movie theater or movie lobby when we least expect it? Why not enjoy the mingling of such an encounter and cherish it as a gift from the dead?

# Chapter Seven:
## MISSOURI

As an important, contested state during the American Civil War where several bloody battles were fought, Missouri was the gateway to the American West. With its strong history of paranormal happenings, UFO sightings, and a variety of things that go bump in the night, it remains an important area for paranormal and UFO investigation.

Missouri has seen an increase in UFO activity since 2002, and appears to continue to be an ongoing point of interest for extraterrestrials and their UFO landings.

There are many famous people connected with the state of Missouri, including William Least Heat-Moon, Laura Ingalls Wilder, Calamity Jane, Tennessee Williams, Robert A. Heinlein, Emmett Kelly, Josephine Baker, Muriel Battle, Jane Froman, Carry A. Nation, Rose O'Neill, Sacred Sun, Margaret Bush Wilson, Langston Hughes, Mark Twain, Sally Rand, Kathleen Turner, Don Cheadle, Scott Bakula, Frank Converse, Walt Disney, Andreas Katsulas, Sandahl Bergman, Kevin Kline, Sara Evans, Chuck Berry, Craig Stevens, William Powell, Sheryl Crow, Vance Randolph, Margaret Truman, Eminen, William Burroughs, Harry S. Truman, Big Soldier, T. S. Eliot, John Goodman, Edwin Hubble, Betty Grable, Walter Cronkite, Vincent Price, Red Foxx, Pearl White, Jesse James, Frank James, Cole Younger, Bob Barker, Stan Musial, Lester Dent, Maya Angelou, Rush Limbaugh, John Huston, Dick Gregory, Dennis Weaver, Andy Williams, Casey Stengel, Roy Wilkins, Brad Pitt, Ginger Rogers, Dick Van Dyke, Virgil Thomson, Sara Teasdale, Thomas Hart Benton, Satchel Paige, Helen Stephens, George Caleb Bingham, George Washington Carver, Annie Turnbo Malone, Dred Scott, Daniel Boone, Rebecca Bryan Boone, Nathan Boone, Marlin Perkins, Yogi Berra, Charlie "Bird" Parker, Scott Joplin, John Joseph Pershing, Omar Nelson Bradley, Dale Carnegie, Marianne Moore, Geraldine

Page, Wallace Berry, J. C. Penney, Robert Altman, Grace Bumbry, Eugene Field, Robert Cummings, Jeanne Eagels, Burt Bacharach, Jane Darwell, and William Wells Brown.

# BLUE SPRINGS

Blue Springs, Missouri, is the site of the Old Lobb Cemetery, which is located in Jackson County, Missouri. Burials commenced in the graveyard in the early 1840s. It is an old cemetery with reports of much vandalism and stealing of grave markers.

Hauntings include:

† A young boy walking in the cemetery, and a teenage girl walking in the back part of the cemetery.
† Two American Civil War ghosts reportedly haunt the perimeters of the cemetery; both are Confederate soldiers who died in that war.
† A woman is heard crying near the entrance to the cemetery, but no one is there to be seen!

# EXCELSIOR SPRINGS

A pleasant, friendly city in Missouri, Excelsior Springs has a most intriguing history behind its hauntings. The small city is located approximately thirty miles northeast of Kansas City, Missouri. The why and the how go together to make this a hotbed for ghost hunters. The ghosts of those who came here over the decades seeking to be healed by the water in the springs haunt the town.

The healing properties of the spring water were discovered in 1880, and later scientific analysis confirmed the unusual mineral properties of the water as a healing elixir. The spring water contains bicarbonates of iron, manganese, Lithia, and other minerals.

The city's many haunted locations include:

† The Elms Hotel has many ghost stories attached to it. Originally constructed in 1888, the Elms Hotel was destroyed by fire twice. It was rebuilt a third time in 1912.

† The bridge over Fishing River on Marietta Street is said to have ghostly visitors, and the historical structure known as the Hall of Waters is now home to the many city offices of Excelsior Springs.

† There are twenty known springs in the area, including Siloam Springs. Siloam Mountain Park covers twenty-five acres, gives excellent access to the city, and has three unique gazebos.

† Excelsior Springs Hospital is reportedly haunted by shadow figures, which have also been seen on Joy Street.

† On August 6, 1925 the wrongful lynching of Walter Mitchell for rape took place; however, it was discovered he did not rape the woman. His ghost reportedly haunts the area where he was hanged and elsewhere in the city.

† In 1931, a gun battle took place at the Elms Hotel between four robbers and the police.

† In 1932, a gangster named Lonnie Affronti shot Azalea Ross and her husband on Route 10, and one of Affronti's cohorts, Charley Harvey, was captured. He committed suicide in the city jail, but his ghost still, reputedly, haunts the city.

† Jesse James' ghost has been seen walking down Jesse James Road in the west side of the city.

† Other ghosts from different eras inhabit the city — alongside its living inhabitants!

# Kansas City

A race of beings, or creatures, known as the lizard people live and dwell next to humans in Kansas City, Missouri. These lizard people are of different types and are reported to live on the outskirts of the city, in its tunnels and underground passages, within the scattered caves found in the county, and inside river way passage entrances. The lizard people have been known to shape-shift into human form and do so to conceal their true identity when mingling with humans! These lizard people have been seen and encountered throughout the state of Missouri, and there have been ongoing conflicts between them and humans since after the close of World War II, although sightings of these creatures are said to originate in Missouri as long ago as the beginning of the 1920s.

The paranormal and UFO connections surrounding these lizard people have not been discovered at this time, but open sightings have become more prevalent since the 1990s. The lizard people are said to resemble humans in form with the difference being they have lizard-like skin over their bodies and private parts, and their faces resemble that of a lizard. Stories about the rape and abduction of human females by lizard people have circulated since the 1970s.

No lizard people remains have been found and documented as of this writing, but armed conflict between them and humans has occurred. A documented report of one type of this lizard race was at Mount Vernon, Missouri, where the actual sighting happened in 1983. Readers may recall the popular television series about lizard extraterrestrials, titled "V," and how one form of alien lizard people may appear physically. An updated version of "V" debuted on television November 3, 2009 starring Morena Baccarin in the role of the lizard leader that arrives on earth. The original miniseries (1983) and series (1984–1985) of the same title starred actor Marc Singer in the role of the human fighting the lizards.

## Union Cemetery

Kansas City, Missouri, is a lively, old city with something for everybody. A visit to Union Cemetery is a must for anyone interested in the paranormal and ghost hauntings. Located at 227 East 28th Terrace, this cemetery will intrigue you from the moment you arrive until the moment you leave. According to records, Union Cemetery was the first recognized public cemetery in Kansas City.

This cemetery is large, but you can walk it in a full day, becoming involved with reading the grave markers of the those interned below your feet. There are over 55,000 graves, including soldiers from the American Civil War. Stories of their ghosts being seen have been reported. A group of seven Union soldiers in military uniform were seen visiting together, talking, their lips moving and laughing in silence. Upon approach, two of the soldiers stopped talking and looked directly at the living visitors. The soldiers then vanished... this has happened before.

Also, an elderly couple has been seen walking together in the western section of the cemetery. Dressed in 1930s clothing, they seem oblivious to their surroundings, smiling and intent on each other's company. It is as if they are out for a stroll.

Sounds of music have been heard in this cemetery too. If you listen carefully, you will discover it is an invisible ghost band with a lead trumpet; the music being played is 1940s style.

There are also famous people buried within this cemetery — it's fun to discover who is interred here.

### Orbs and Mists

If you are interested in orbs, this cemetery will definitely surprise you with its seemingly unending number of them.

There are also an abundance of shadow figures that hover just out of range and fade away upon approach. Is this cemetery haunted? Yes, it is, and like some cemeteries where there is much paranormal activity, there are areas where mists form. It is not unusual to see a mist form around a certain grave, or perhaps, two graves. Some mists form over several graves and linger there, as if in a form of silent communion with each other.

### Other Hauntings

† The voice of a man singing in French can be heard.

† A child has been seen running in the south section — only to disappear as he turns the corner of a marker.

† The following apparitions have been reported: an elderly gentleman dressed in a suit and bowler hat of the Edwardian era; a young woman wearing a blue dress and standing motionless in front of a burial plot; a dog running and jumping across graves vanishes in mid-air; and a white cat runs towards the living — only to meow and disappear a few feet away; an Asian man points to the sky and smiles before vanishing into a mist; two ladies dressed in Victorian era clothing leisurely chat together as they walk arm-in-arm towards a gravesite and vanish at its base; two young sisters play chase and laugh; and a man dressed in 1880s western clothing with boots and a cowboy hat stares thoughtfully at you and then fades slowly away until there is no trace of him anywhere.

† The smells of cinnamon and cigar smoke from an invisible smoker have been detected in the air.

† The sound of an owl have been heard, though no owl is in sight.

These are only a few of the reputed hauntings available to the living visitor who has the time to savor the setting. You are in for a personal treat when you visit this old cemetery. There is no telling what haunting variations you will encounter. See what you connect with — you may be very surprised!

## *Other City Hauntings*

### The Missouri River

With a long and colorful history, there are stories of bobbing heads in the river that submerge and never resurface. Another haunting is that of a flatboat containing Confederate soldiers in the middle of the river. There is a scene played out on the banks of the river's north side where a group of Union and Confederate soldiers are firing rifles at each other, but this ghostly scene fades and vanishes upon approach.

### Penn Valley Park

Located at 31st and Main Streets across from Crown Center and within walking distance of Union Station, Penn Valley is a quiet, scenic park — reputed to have not only shadow figures on the grounds, but also some solid ghosts of female and male appearance. These include the ghosts of elderly couples who have been seen to appear and then fade into nothingness at sunset.

### Swope Park

With approximately 1,763 acres, Swope Park is a scenic beauty spot. It, reputedly, has a haunted lake where odd things have been seen in the water along the shoreline. Shadow figures have been seen in the picnic areas, and the ghost of a young man dressed in 1960s clothing reportedly haunts the amphitheater.

### Union Station

Located at 30 West Pershing Road, Union Station is one of the most interesting historical locations to visit. Built in 1914, it encompasses 850,000 square feet, and was successfully renovated in 1999. The Grand Hall contains three, magnificent 3,500-pound chandeliers. Amtrak stops there.

As a cultural location, it also contains fine restaurants and gift shops. The Union Café is found in the Grand Hall under the giant clock, and other eating places include the Harvey House Diner, Pierport's, and the Times Square Concessionaire. If you are looking for a sampling of Kansas City's fine steaks, try the steak dinner at Pierport's located in the northeast corner of Grand Hall. I would recommend the tasty, delicious breakfast omelets available at the Harvey House Diner in the east end of the Grand Hall.

Given its nature as a transportation center over the decades, it is no surprise to find hauntings and ghosts there. Many incidents of soldier ghosts have occurred, and those are primarily of the World War II era. A World War I soldier, in complete doughboy uniform and carrying a rifle over his soldier, was reputed to have been a fixture at the entrance of Union Station prior to World War II.

# St. Louis

Wonderfully haunted, St. Louis, Missouri, is one of the most interesting older cities in the United States. There is always something to entertain visitors!

Caves are always a possible location for ghosts and paranormal activity, some more so than others. Despite the best efforts of Hollywood movies, newly discovered caves do not necessarily have some evil thing lurking within them, but some caves do have residual hauntings. Possibly some have intelligent hauntings.

Any underground location that contains a cave or a maze of caves does have the possibility of paranormal incidents. I would suggest to the reader that a fascinating book could be written about the paranormal connected with caves and it would be a very thick book. As for St. Louis, it does have caves.

The possibility that under the city of St. Louis is a maze of connecting and non-connecting caves is highly likely. Historically, St. Louis beer makers utilized many caves and huge cavern areas for breweries. The Lemp family of St. Louis had such access to caverns and made ready use of the built-in coolness. Caves made for easy cool storage, and limited the spoilage of perishable goods. St. Louis is much like Springfield in the sense that both cities are built upon caves, and there are more unknown caves than there are known ones.

I was told by three different people, including a geologist and a biologist, that for every known cave in Missouri, there are at least five unknown, undiscovered, and forgotten caves still to be found. Other people have given me other educated guesses as to the possible number of caves still to be discovered in Missouri. That is a large number of unknown caves just waiting to be found. However, most of these caves will never be found, so I have been told. Alas, there goes my dream of one day owning a cave in Missouri — although I am reasonably sure there is one somewhere deep beneath my feet and chair as I sit writing these very words!

The history of caves makes for a wonderful look at the ingenuity of humans putting caves to use over the many thousands of years. If there does come a climatic or terrorist holocaust, caves will be of prime importance for survival. If that becomes the case, humans should be aware that they would be sharing space with the ghosts of the cave's past to some degree, depending upon how haunted the cave is.

As to the underground cave system in St. Louis, there are some well-known caves.

## Cherokee Cave

Not only was this cave utilized by Adam Lemp for his brewery, but also for his personal use. With the passage of time and social changes, Cherokee Cave was sold and opened to the public for tours by a man named Lee Hess and featured such sights as the Spaghetti Room and the Petrified Falls, but in 1961 the cave complex was sold to the Missouri Highway Department and permanently closed. Was it forgotten and no longer able to be entered? To the diehard cave searcher, no. There are ways into the cave. The Lemp Theater is still there among other relics. Haunted? Some say yes. Shadow figures are said to be there. What else, one wonders?

## English Cave

Originally owned by Ezra O. English in 1826, English Cave is a well-documented cave with a history of paranormal activity. Now filled with

water and inaccessible, English Cave was the site of the St. Louis Brewery in 1839. English Cave is, reputedly, haunted by different entities, including American Indians and victims of the cholera epidemic that devastated the city in 1849.

There is a story told of a young couple in love that fled into English Cave and died inside it rather than be separated. The couple's ghosts are said to haunt the depths of English Cave and strange, eerie voices were frequently heard here. A feeling of the macabre permeates what is known as English Cave.

### Caves as Breweries?

Uhrig's Cave served as a base for beer brewery operations. Another known cave used for brewery operations, now permanently sealed off from public access, is called the Sidney Street Cave.

~~~~~

Other caves await discovery in St. Louis, Missouri. What is lurking inside them, I wonder?

# SPRINGFIELD

One of the most haunted cities in the state of Missouri is Springfield. With the bloody Battle of Wilson's Creek during the American Civil War, the area takes on an even more macabre sense of being haunted by things dead, unseen, and reaching out to touch somebody!

The Confederate Cemetery section is known to be haunted, as are other places in the National Cemetery. I have walked the cemetery and have felt and seen the presence of ghosts. There are many of them.

Known in southern history as the Battle of Oak Hills, the American Civil War's Battle at Wilson's Creek, ten miles south of Springfield, was a hard-fought victory for the Confederacy. Located at 6424 West Farm Road 182 near Republic, Missouri, it was a bloody battle with extreme numbers of wounded on both sides — 1,317 Union soldiers were killed and 1,222 Confederate soldiers. No historical documents exist that reveal how many more died on both sides from injuries and wounds received during the fighting. The battle took place August 10, 1861, and is historically important as the first major battle of the American Civil War west of the Mississippi River.

The bloody battle also witnessed the death of Union general, Nathaniel Lyon. Missouri ranks third as the most fought over state during the war. Although its sympathy was with the South and it had a keen wish to remain neutral, Missouri became a bloodbath for both sides.

Maintained today by the National Park Service, the area of battle is noted for its excellent shape and has become a visitor site favorite. Ongoing archaeological digs and new finds continually turn up relics from the bloody encounter. Like much of the Springfield area in general, there are relics still to be found and much that is buried deep in the soil or covered by soil and structures. There are stories of buried weapons, rifles, ammunition, and money, not yet found. One of the more famous stories is that a wagon carried rifles wrapped in heavy protective cloth, and was buried to insure its secret location before the battle. To this day, it has never been found, and remains an elusive mystery to be solved.

Ghost stories abound concerning Wilson's Creek and its surrounding area. Numerous accounts of residual hauntings have been shared privately and publicly since the battle was fought. Many sightings of

ghost soldiers involved in this famous battle have been seen, and there is indeed an eerie feeling about the place. That feeling is intensified with the approach of evening — evening time at Wilson's Creek battlefield is the time of the shadow figures.

The American Civil War has inspired much paranormal literature, including fiction, nonfiction, and movies. Those interested in pursuing this research will find much to intrigue and entertain them!

The Springfield Public Square, or The Square as old-time residents affectionately call it, has a checkered history that is both interesting and important. John Polk Campbell donated the acreage for the public square in 1835 and the first courthouse was built in the center section of this square. During 1858 the Butterfield Overland Stage established a stop point route there.

As the American Civil War got underway, the state was torn between North and South control. Colonel Franz Sigel with his Union troops arrived at the square on June 24, 1861, and troops extended their excursions into North Springfield. By August, the Confederate soldiers led by General Sterling Price seized control of the square. On October 25, 1861, a skillful raid led by Union troops under command of Major Charles Zagonyi resulted in the burning and destruction of the square courthouse. During 1862 and 1863, both the North and South attempted to secure Springfield for its own use. Confederate forces were overcome and driven back by the Union soldiers on January 8, 1863.

The Square continues in importance as a historical hub for Springfieldians, and during 1970 the area was named Park Central Square. Much of The Square has been renovated and the old buildings refurbished.

One interesting building on the public square is the seven-story Heer's Store, which was originally built in 1869. Constructed for use as a department store, it was solidly built with steel, terra cotta, wood, and concrete. It had 100,000 feet of usable floor space. Ravaged by fire, it was rebuilt during 1915. The Heer's building had a long, prosperous life until it went out of business in 1995. This old landmark structure is being restored, and renovated in 2008.

There are other old buildings on the public square and in the immediate surrounding area, including the Holland Building and the Woodruff Building. Visitors to the Springfield Public Square will find it fascinating.

## Fassnight Park

Located at Meadowmere and South Campbell avenues, next to Parkview High School, is Fassnight Park. Conrad and Emma Fassnight sold twenty-eight acres of land in 1924 to the city of Springfield. This land included trees and a creek. Over a period of years, under the direction and guidance of a stonemason named Godfrey Messerli, the bathhouse, pool, bridges, and other structures were completed as part of a project by the Works Progress Administration. During 1977, the pool and structures were renovated.

A persistent story since the 1930s was that there existed small openings to caves in the Fassnight Park bluffs, and they were dynamited to seal these entrances off from children entering them. My examination of these rock formations revealed to me that there could have been such cave openings and the openings were collapsed. With the passage of time, fact mixes with rumor and it becomes difficult to ascertain if there were cave openings. Given the nature of the Missouri cave system and its many connections, it is highly possible the cave openings were a fact. As a child I played and went swimming in this park often.

### The Bathhouse

The bathhouse is considered haunted. There have been ghost stories over the years of swimmers entering the bathhouse, seeing another person there — and then that person is suddenly gone. Shadow figures have also been seen near the bathhouse; they vanish upon approach. Peals of rowdy laughter have been heard inside the bathhouse when nobody is there.

There are three other ghost stories of merit:

† The appearance of a young, dark-haired woman wearing a short purple dress is seen during the twilight hours; she is leaning over the metal fence railing at the top of the stairs, looking down at the park.
† Another haunting is that of a young man wearing a black swimsuit looking out from the bathhouse balcony across the swimming pool.

†An elderly woman dressed in 1940s clothes is reputed to be waving at some person in the park from her vantage point at the top of the stairs; she is facing the left bridge.

An interesting aspect of these residual hauntings is their quick appearance and disappearance, and different people have seen different things over the decades.

## The Bridges

Two young women in love, strolling hand in hand, together have been seen crossing the bridges; they walk over the bridges and vanish at the other end. This couple is seen during the early winter months. They are wearing long coats, dressed for cool weather, and wearing stocking caps. Age wise, they appear to be in their early thirties. They show no recognition of the living as they peacefully stroll together. The appearance of these two women ghosts is that of a residual haunting.

I personally spent a lot of time in this old park, and I am aware of its enduring charm and haunted nature. I have seen the ghost of the young woman wearing a short purple dress.

## *Pythian Castle*

A legendary building containing paranormal occurrences at the park is Pythian Castle. There are many stories that have flourished over the decades about this unusual place, originally constructed by the Knights of Pythias as an orphanage in 1913. The Knights of Pythias were a charitable organization and much information is available about it, including material found on the Internet.

Later, the building and land was purchased and owned by the United States military and used for German soldier internment during World War II. It is rumored that some of these prisoners of war were tortured during confinement and some died.

My first encounter with the haunted Pythian Castle was in 1956 when I went there with my Uncle Willard. I do not recall why we went there, but I recall vividly what happened to me. Inside the entrance, somebody touched my face and I could not see anything that did the touching. Then I heard a woman's gentle voice beside me, but I could see nothing and nobody except my Uncle Willard and I who were standing inside the entrance. At the time of contact, I felt a sudden chill pass through my body but nothing else. That is all that I recall of the ghostly encounter, and it does remain a vivid, early memory of being part of a haunting.

Over the nearly hundred years of existence, ghostly experiences have been spoken about or passed on from one generation to another. These hauntings include being touched by something not seen, bumping into a mass but not seeing anything, a mass bumping into a person or persons on its way to somewhere, an abundance of orbs, quick temperature changes, doors shutting by themselves, furniture moving by itself, a variety children and adult voices, laughter, a woman weeping, a man weeping, strange mists that form and vanish, and the sound of a meowing cat running upstairs.

A terrifying documentary was filmed about Pythian Castle and other hauntings titled "Children of the Grave," by the well-known filmmakers, Philip Adrian Booth and Christopher Saint Booth. It was released as a DVD in 2007. Scary in the true sense of the word, this documentary will have you sitting on the edge of your seat as you watch it unfold and wonder what horror is coming along next to confront you! There is shocking ghost footage that will scare the viewers with its intensity. Anybody wishing to see a ninety-minute film version about some of Missouri's hauntings and scary places will find this a great item to own and view frequently.

## The Paranormal in Movies and Books

For those interested in an entertaining 1950s look at occurrences based on true paranormal events should view the old black & white television series, "One Step Beyond" (1959–1961) with guest host, John Newland. A new DVD release, featuring the best fifty complete episodes, was released in 2007 on a special four-CD collection. Among the numerous actors and actresses of this highly popular television series were Christopher Lee, Elizabeth Montgomery, Mike Connors, Yvette Mimieux, Suzanne Pleshette, Ross Martin, Norma Crane, Robert Loggia, Joanne Linville, Charles Bronson, Albert Salmi, Patrick O'Neal, Peggy Ann Garner, Robert Webber, Louise Fletcher, Patrick Macnee, Elen Willard, George Grizzard, Barbara Lord, Richard Devon, and Cloris Leachman.

There are many movies available for watching, among them the critically-acclaimed "The Legend of Hell House" (1973) starring Pamela Franklin, Roddy McDowall, Clive Revill, and Gayle Hunnicutt, and "Stephen King's Rose Red" (2002) starring Julian Sands, Nancy Travis, Matt Keeslar, and David Dukes. Additional selections to consider might be "The Shining" (1980) with Jack Nicholson and Shelly Duvall, "The Changeling" (1979) with George C. Scott and Trish Van Devere, "The Ghost Goes West" (1936) with Robert Donat and Jean Parker, "Ghostbusters" (1984) starring Bill Murray, Dan Aykroyd, and Sigourney Weaver, "The Ghost and Mrs. Muir" (1947) with Rex Harrison and Gene Tierney, "Ghost" (1990) with Patrick Swayze and Demi Moore.

Some of humankind's greatest fears about hauntings, ghosts, and the macabre have been played out on film. Fiction writers have utilized these fears for decades, and such writings are too many to list, but a few are *The Uninhabited House*, *Ghosts in Daylight*, *A Phantom Lover*, *Ghost Story*, *The Beckoning Fair One*, *Widdershins*, *The Turn of the Screw*, *A Christmas Carol*, *They Return at Evening*, and *The Lady in White*.

As long as humans feel fear and excitement about the paranormal, there will be filmmakers and writers to fuel that fear and excitement with their creative efforts! Some efforts will undoubtedly be more enjoyable and better crafted than others, which is true of any legitimate art form, but it would be interesting to see what kind of movie could be made about Pythian Castle with an acting cast to match!

## *Fox Theater*

The building that was once the Fox Theater is located on the Springfield Public Square. It opened in 1916. Many people have said it is built upon an entrance to the cave running to and connecting with Doling Park. I recall my Uncle Willard telling me that there was a bank vault in the basement of the theater that contained European paintings from the 1930s era, and was actually built into the cave opening and used to seal the cave entrance.

Uncle Willard did not allow me to sit in the balcony because he believed it was not a good place to be. There have been stories of ghostly presences in the basement and the balcony. Located on the northeast corner of the Springfield Public Square, it remains a fine personal memory to me, for, as a child, I went to see many, many movies there.

I recall going to a Saturday showing and the western cowboy actor, Randolph Scott, was there. Randolph Scott (1898–1987) was a fine actor from North Carolina who was also a Freemason and active in the York Rite. Among his classic movies were "The Virginian" (1929), "Supernatural" (1933), "Roberta" and "She" (1935), "Seven Men from Now" (1955), "Tall T" (1956), and "Ride the High Country" (1962). I remember seeing Scott on stage and hearing him speak to the happy, loud audience. Later, I shook his hand in the theater lobby in front of the wall murals; the mural depicting the American Civil War battle at Wilson's Creek, to be exact. These murals are registered historic landmarks.

While living in Santa Monica Canyon, California, in the 1960s, I came into contact again with Randolph Scott attending a movie with fellow actor Wendell Corey (1914–1968). I went up to him, re-introduced myself, and shook his hand again. I told him I was living in Santa Monica Canyon not far from the home of my friends, novelist Christopher Isherwood and his companion, artist Don Bachardy. Scott and I visited and then went our separate ways. Randolph Scott was truly one of the most gracious, polite people you could ever hope to encounter; he had a sense of Southern class about him that was impeccable. His voice, smile, and handshake were sincere. Randolph Scott made some of the finest American Western films in movie history — and he may still be visiting the Fox Theater at some ghostly matinee!

Today, the Fox Theater is a pleasant church setting owned by the Abundant Life Covenant Church. This positive, enjoyable religious house is a nice place to attend services, and they publish their own religious magazine titled *Present Truth*. Debra and I both felt the gentle peacefulness of this congregation, and we had the good fortune of encountering numerous scenes of past times that took place on the stage in the large auditorium. The stage had psychic images of a positive nature that Debra and I both comfortably witnessed. These were definitely residual images — more along the lines of a history tour with the psychic images from the past marching along at a fast clip. One particular scene Debra and I both shared was the psychic image of the theater seats being filled with children intently watching a movie on the screen!

The original J. C. Penney building was located next to the Fox Theater, as was a clothing store named Barth's. This corner of The Square is considered highly haunted. Rumors of ghostly encounters and cold spots in the bathrooms, basement, and other areas of the old J. C. Penny building have been reputed over the years. Nothing harmful has taken place there, but rather people having encounters with presences and hearing voices.

### Phelps Grove Park

Phelps Grove Park is located at 950 East Bennett in Springfield. It has thirty-one acres, which includes a xeriscape garden and a long stone pavilion building. The toilet facilities are considered haunted in the pavilion and laughter has been heard there. The laughter is not loud and can be either male or female. No sign of bodies…just ghost voices. Shadow figures have been seen in the stone pavilion building.

# JOPLIN

A mining city with a history of paranormal encounters since it was established, Joplin, Missouri, is like many mining towns in American history -- it had colorful, rugged, and sometimes violent episodes in its past. Famous for its zinc and lead mines, the area was originally opened up for settlement before the American Civil War. Today, Joplin is a busy setting with a growing population and offers many activities for visitors, even though its haunted Crystal Cave was long ago filled in and a permanent parking lot built over it!

Growing up in Missouri, I heard many unusual stories about hauntings and ghosts in Joplin. Located in the southwestern corner of Missouri, situated at approximately 1,000 feet elevation on thirty square miles of land, the city of Joplin was at one time considered the lead and zinc capitol of the world. It was named after Reverend Harris Joplin who founded the first major Methodist congregation and church in the city. Lead mining started before the American Civil War, and by 1871 there was a large abundance of mining camps in operation. Joplin as a city became recognized in 1873.

Mining was discontinued in the late 1940s and completely closed in the early 1950s, the maze of tunnels abandoned. One intriguing aspect of Joplin is the startling fact that seventy-five percent of its land, houses, buildings, structures, and streets are undermined by the tunnels beneath the city. These old mine tunnels still exist and it is not uncommon to discover houses whose basements have a door opening into a mine for which the miner could come and go at random, going to work and returning home from work. Most of these entrances to mine tunnels are closed or permanently sealed, but they are still intact to some degree.

That these tunnels are haunted and have paranormal activity is something most ghost hunters would like to investigate more openly. Yet, the risk of mine cave-ins and other problems now existing with these old tunnels, mine shafts, and mines make it a highly hazardous undertaking that has not been done. The passage of time has done much to permanently make these mines off limits for paranormal explorations. Oronogo and Webb City are two small towns close to Joplin noted for mines and tunnels.

More recently, a massive tornado struck Joplin May 5, 1971. The center of the city was devastated.

Joplin is famous for some of its structures, among them, the House of Lords. The House of Lords was a famous saloon, and contained a restaurant area, gambling tables, and an active upper floor used for prostitution and other sexual pursuits. Other interesting places included the Schifferdecker House built in 1890, and the Joplin Suppy Company building.

Famous figures associated with Joplin include Bonnie and Clyde, who lived in a hideout here for several weeks in the 1930s; they robbed several local businesses. Their stay ended in a shoot-out, but this famous outlaw couple escaped Joplin without injury. Stories of the ghostly presences of Bonnie and Clyde in Joplin still circulate.

Robert Cummings (1910–1990) was a famous actor from Joplin, as was actor Dennis Weaver (1924–2006). Famous writer and poet Langston Hughes (1902–1967) also came from Joplin.

Joplin is noted for its friendly atmosphere and good meals. I would suggest the visitor try one of the restaurants offering roast beef, scalloped potatoes in gravy sauce, French green beans, sourdough toast, coffee, and apple pie or home-made bread pudding with vanilla sauce. It is always an enjoyment to visit Joplin when the opportunity presents itself.

## Haunted Locations

With its rough and rowdy early history adding to its appeal, there can be no doubt that there are haunted places in this old mining town, including the Joplin Supply Company.

Originally built in 1899 at Fourth Street, the Joplin Supply Company is located downtown on what is today called Michigan Avenue. An old building with a long history in the city, it reputedly has a woman's ghost on the fourth floor. The ghost of a smiling, pretty young child has also been seen staring out of a second floor window.

### The Schifferdecker Home

Located on Sargeant Avenue, the Schifferdecker Home was built in 1890 and is in excellent shape. Orbs have been seen in the windows of the attic, as has a shadow figure, much like a man.

Voices have been heard in the house, but no bodies have been seen to connect with those voices. An interesting place, it makes for a unique visit. There is a pleasant feel about the house.

### Shoal Creek

A band of American Indians on a hunting expedition have been seen in the Shoal Creek and Grand Falls area near Joplin, Missouri. An American Indian riding a brown horse is reputed to appear at different places along the creek banks, as if studying the terrain or searching for something on the ground. Perhaps, he is tracking an animal or in pursuit of a person.

Shadow figures have appeared near the banks of the creek, only to step back and vanish at the approach of humans. Bobbing heads have been seen in the water. These bobbing heads submerge and do not resurface. The heads of two young men have been seen, but vanish upon approach.

A young black-haired woman with fair complexion is seen floating on her back; she is wearing a one-piece red swimsuit and seems to be resting. Upon closer examination, she vanishes below the surface, fades away, and is not seen again.

### Wildcat Glades Park

Also located near Joplin, Missouri, Wildcat Glades Park is a lovely, scenic park setting, with a sense of quiet that is breathtaking and relaxing. Opened fully to the public in 2007, the park contains chert trails for hikers to explore. It is also a nature center for conservation, and an Audubon Center due to its variety of bird species.

It has shadow figures, and a white ghost horse is said to prowl its boundaries. The ghost horse carries the ghost of a young girl wearing a long white dress. A throaty laughter without a presence to be seen has also occurred. This laughter appears in the western section of Wildcat Glades Park. It is the sound of a male ghost.

# BRANSON

The ghost of Cameron Mitchell resides here in Branson, Missouri. Mitchell (1918–1994) was a very popular American film, radio, television, and Broadway actor with an active career that spanned from 1945 until his death. Many people remember him in the role of Uncle Buck Cannon in the popular television series, "The High Chaparral." The series ran from 1967–1971 and was set in the American West; this character role was one that Cameron Mitchell appeared to enjoy and excelled in.

A prolific film and television star, Cameron Mitchell's character roles were interesting and varied. Although references vary, it is estimated Mitchell made over 200 movies during his career. Here is a quick reference guide to some of his films: "They Were Expendable" (1945), "Adventures of Gallant Bess" (1948), "Death of a Salesman" and "Flight to Mars" (1951), "Pony Soldier" and "Les Miserables" (1952), "Man on a Tight Rope," "How to Marry a Millionaire," and "The Robe" (1953;

he was the voice of Jesus Christ in the latter), "Garden of Evil" (1954), "House of Bamboo" and "Love Me or Leave Me" (1955), "Carousel" and "Tension at Table Rock" (1956), "All Mine to Give" and "Monkey On My Back" (1957; the latter is considered one of his finest film roles), "The Tall Men" and "Pier 5, Havana" (1959), "Caesar the Conqueror" (1962), "Minnesota Clay" (1965), "Hombre" (1967), "Nightmare in Wax" (1969), "Buck and the Preacher" and "The Other Side of the Wind" (1972), "The Klansman," "The Hanged Man" , and "The Midnight Man" (1974), "The Guns and the Fury" (1981), "My Favorite Year" (1982), "Prince Jack" (1985), "The Tomb" (1986), and "Jack–O" (1995).

Cameron Mitchell's ghost has been seen at different restaurants and gift shops in the historic business section of Branson. First seen in Branson during the summer of 2000, Mitchell's ghost is seen wearing a dark business suit and is smiling.

## *Branson Scenic Railway*

There are many ghostly walkers at the Branson Scenic Railway. Perhaps it is the area itself, or the land upon which these structures were built, but there are ghostly presences there. This depot was built near the White River in 1905; the Railway takes passengers through the foothills of the lovely Ozark Mountains. Along the way, passengers will have a great opportunity to see wilderness areas and the remains of deserted communities. Some of the deserted communities include Gretna, Melva, and Ruth, which can be seen as the train meanders along the tracks of what was originally known as the White River Railway. Today it is known as the White River Route.

As to ghosts found at the depot, some images are much more detailed than others, such as the couple dressed in 1930s clothes taking a leisurely stroll or the small boy with a walking stick laughing at the sky. As they did not seek contact, I would define them as residual hauntings. Visiting with people in the area, it seems this is a place where spooks can appear at anytime, but generally during evening hours.

The intriguing aspect of railroad sites, trains, and rails is that over the decades they have become notorious for hauntings, ghosts, paranormal occurrences, and supernatural situations, which also accounts for their enduring popularity and curiosity. Many people have paranormal tales to share about railroad locations, and there have been documented accounts of ghosts seen at such places throughout the world. Intelligent hauntings and residual hauntings abound. My wife Debra saw a tall woman with a long dress near the platform. She said this ghost was there for a few seconds and then vanished. I saw an elderly man dressed in the style of the 1940s staring into the distance towards the river… he was gone after less than a minute.

As people train themselves to prepare for anything they encounter in the paranormal as coming of its own biding, they will also find it can and will happen with more frequency. When you have fears, you sometimes block out what you seek to discover. Be alert to your senses. Train and rely on your intuition. Hauntings can occur when you least expect them to, but when they appear, investigate the moment at hand for all that it offers you as an intimate glimpse into the world of the paranormal. Although some people may feel that all hauntings are the same, I assure this is not the case, for each haunting has its own characteristics and points of reference. With the passage of time, you will become more experienced in meeting the paranormal. You will also come to appreciate the differences discovered with individual hauntings! These differences make for memorable encounters.

## Old Matt's Cabin

A landmark site at Branson, Old Matt's Cabin is haunted. There have been ghost and paranormal stories surrounding this cabin seemingly forever and, depending upon whom you speak, you will be surprised by what you hear! Not only is the ghost of writer Harold Bell Wright reputed to haunt the area, but also there is something strange about the cabin and its location. It is something you can sense when you are in close proximity. Whether or not a heaviness of electricity in the air, or the approach of a pending storm has some influence, it is hard to say or prove. Shadow figures have been seen around the cabin during the day, and the weather conditions at the time of their appearances may be normal, cold, wet, windy, or otherwise. My feeling is that weather does not have a direct bearing in this particular situation at Old Matt's Cabin because what is there has been there a long time!

Just as a ghost investigator may not feel drops in temperatures with a sensation of coldness or a rise in temperature with a sensation of warmness, that may also apply to seeing shadow figures in all types of situations or weather settings. Simply put, a lot depends on the ghost, and whether the ghost is a residual haunting or an intelligent haunting. I have encountered my share of temperature fluctuations. Heat fluctuations, whether hot or cold changes in temperatures, are secondary to other factors. Not everybody feels fluctuations in temperatures when encountering a haunting, paranormal situation, or ghosts. It depends on the person and the ghostly situation being examined.

Historically, J. K. Ross was the builder of the cabin, which is named after its builder. Harold Bell Wright's book, *The Shepherd of the Hills*, published in 1907, made the Ross cabin and the Branson area famous, as Branson and Old Matt's Cabin became international sites to visit. A silent black and white movie version of the book was made and released in 1919 and, although movie lobby cards of it still exist, there are no known film prints in existence. A Technicolor movie version of this famous novel was released to theaters in 1941 starring John Wayne, Betty Field, Beulah Bondi, James Barton, and Harry Carey; the movie version differed from the book version. A thirty-minute television special was released in 1959, and another film version came out in movie theaters in 1964 starring Richard Arlen.

In 1982, the National Register of Historic Places placed the Ross House in its records and identified it as a national historic landmark. The log structure was originally built in 1895; at approximately fourteen feet by twenty feet in size and square in its design, the log house is almost perfectly square, as numerous people have observed. A frame bedroom and kitchen at the west side was a later addition to the cabin. It is well preserved. Over the many decades it has had different owners.

In 1960, an outdoor drama following the book version was introduced as "The Shepherd of the Hills Outdoor Drama" and continues to entertain audiences today; over the decades, its live performances have continued to grow in popularity. The Shepherd of the Hills Theater is located at 5586 West Highway 76 in Branson.

On one of my visits to Branson, I visited with a woman who claimed an unusual incident happened to her personally at Old Matt's Cabin; for personal reasons, she requested anonymity, so I will call her "Mary." I told her I was a sensitive investigating the paranormal and ghosts in

Branson, Missouri, and she expressed her views on several paranormal topics and then got around to her story.

Mary explained to me what happened to her one morning in late April 2008. It is one of the most interesting time portal incidents I have come across in recent years. She said she was near the front entrance to Old Matt's Cabin. In front of the door leading into Old Matt's Cabin, a glowing white mist formed and gave way to an oval opening — a portal approximately six feet high and five feet wide. For the most part, its light obscured the cabin porch. She witnessed a young couple emerge from the time portal and walk down the steps onto the lawn. The man and woman were nondescript, dressed in contemporary clothes, and they saw her watching them. The woman raised her hand and pointed at Mary, and it seemed to Mary that this young woman was holding some small silver-like object. Mary was approximately twenty feet away from the couple, and she found she could not move or speak. This couple was quickly followed by nineteen other couples; each couple observed Mary and then walked away. Mary remained staring at the time portal for what seemed like an eternity to her, and then watched as it faded and vanished into nothingness. Old Matt's Cabin was back to the way it was. Mary could move again and there was no numbness or unusual feeling in her body. There was no sign of the twenty couples that had arrived through the time portal. She had no explanation. The whole incident took less than ten minutes, but Mary became a believer in the possibilities of time travel, dimensional time loops, and paranormal time travel. Who were these people, where did they come from, and why? What was their agenda or purpose?

Time portals, time loops, paranormal time travel, and their related kin is a field of the paranormal that should be examined in-depth! Why, because it is happening, and being witnessed by people! I have always sensed in the presence of Old Matt's Cabin something unusual, a force of some kind that I have never been able to define or explain. I am not so sure it is the cabin itself, as it could also be the immediate area in which the cabin is located. Is it a drop off point for some things that have specific plans, or could it be a focal point for time travel? Is this paranormal time travel or is it something more, perhaps something more sinister or, again, something taking place with a positive intent that is not yet known? Could these time travelers be refugees from some future time? Could this be some previously unknown focal point for UFO teleportation of extraterrestrials to earth, an alien plan of which the human race is unaware of? Could they have been extraterrestrial guides beginning a mission in Missouri?

There are many aspects involved with this sighting, but, at this time, there is no hard evidence to suggest what is what and which is which! I have always felt this particular area was strange even when I first saw it as a child. If you are there long enough, you may feel the sensation that something is not quite in sync with its surroundings and, although it does not cause a sense of déjà vu, unease, or confusion, it is a sensation of curiosity as to what it might be. In a way, the visitor to this area wonders as he or she wanders around!

When you visit this lovely, peaceful, and serene area, ask yourself what it is you are experiencing. Do you have a pleasant feeling that time has stopped, and the gentle peacefulness of the setting is over-powering in its nostalgic appearance? What is most appealing about what you are seeing? What does your mind suggest to you as you look at the cabin and its surroundings? What is just beyond the veil of human perception lurking there? Then ask yourself, what is waiting there, quietly unseen?

# COOMBS FERRY

Not far from Branson is a beautiful area named Coombs Ferry. One of the most unusual places in the state, it is situated between Branson and Kimberling City. Indian Point Park is one mile away and Table Rock State Park is two miles away. Depending on which direction you are coming from, it is less than three to five miles from Branson. In some areas of Coombs Ferry, the water depth is over 100 feet.

In the early 1970s, there was, reportedly, a UFO incident in this area. A UFO disc is reputed to have exploded above the water and scattered its contents and wreckage in the immediate area of water between Coombs Ferry and Indian Point. If anything was found concerning this UFO disc explosion, it was never discussed. If the government stepped in, *nothing* will be discussed. Divers in the area have not revealed any findings, yet it would be interesting to dive the area in a widespread, extensive manner and see what rubble may be there should it still be available for discovery and salvage. This area, known as Table Rock Lake, also includes Jacques Creek, Long Creek, North Indian Creek, and Moonshine Beach.

Coombs Ferry always had an attraction for me; something that was there for me, and I enjoyed visiting it. Depending on my work schedule, I often took dates down there for a picnic lunch, some swimming, rock and fossil hunting, and other pleasant activities. It was a good time and a good place to be with your girl, so to speak, and I have many happy memories of being there with them. It was a good place for family outings, too. All in all, despite the changes time brings to places and people, Coombs Ferry remains a wonderful escape from the hustle and bustle of life!

I knew from my first encounter with this beautiful area that it was haunted. My Uncle Willard agreed. I recall him telling me that he believed the area served other purposes. We both agreed that portals existed in this area, and what might appear to be a flicker of light flashing over a land spot or on the water near shore was like a portal opening and closing. A portal can be as small or as large as you wish within reasonable logic. The age of flying saucers and UFOs became prevalent after World War II, gaining acceptance if not acknowledgment from the many governments of the world. Probably the last government on earth to acknowledge such things will be the United States and only after it has struck up some deal involving money and technology with the aliens. One of the early bases of cooperation between the United States government and extraterrestrials is located at Dulce, New Mexico; it was established there in the 1950s. There are other locations in the great Southwest as well, including Oregon, Missouri, California, Nevada, and Arizona. When I lived in New Mexico, it was not uncommon to see the UFOs, which came in many shapes and sizes. Some people see discs, which are also referred to as disks; others have seen other types of UFOs. In time, other bases will be unmasked and their locations made available. There will come a time when UFOs will arrive in numbers — and no government will be able to dismiss their arrivals as a world mass hallucination.

Any person who claims there are no such things as UFOs is either employed by the government, trying to keep true UFO locations hidden, or afraid of what acknowledgment of UFOs might mean to their personal reality. Most certainly, any person who claims or writes that UFOs are nothing more than a mass world hallucination is ignorant of the documented facts available and definitely should not be given credibility as a reliable witness, writer, or scholar. The paranormal and the occult world have common ground shared with extraterrestrials and UFOs. Some of the oldest writings in Ancient India and other cultures discuss the concept of portals, through which beings and entities from other dimensions can visit our human world. Whether it is a time portal or another dimensional portal connecting our dimension with others, the truth remains that we are not alone, and that is the way of it. Interdimensional beings do exist. It makes no difference in the overall view if it is other-dimensional or inter-dimensional portals; it is the intent of the defined portal that is of paramount importance for the human race.

When I was living at Santa Monica Canyon, California, in the 1960s, my Uncle Willard wrote me letters often and shared his thoughts on many things. One topic of interest was: Angels appearing through portals in time and space and vanishing as quickly as they come after delivering their messages. The same applies to extraterrestrials. Maybe some angels are really extraterrestrials in disguise and that is a readily acceptable costume or disguise they cloak themselves in. Look back over the stories and writings throughout humankind. Think about the possibilities of such things happening. What is a ghost? What is a demon? What is an angel or an extraterrestrial? In what way could each be connected to the other in all the writings since human civilization started writing about such things? We are not alone as a species — we have never been alone.

Coombs Ferry, Missouri is one place to consider for contact, whether it is angels, extraterrestrials, paranormal occurrences, ghosts, or hauntings. Coombs Ferry reaches out across that large lake, connecting with many interesting land features and its nearby human population. I have always believed there is much photographic evidence right before us, buried in old forgotten photo albums or closet shoe boxes, that contain clues to so many things we consider paranormal or extraterrestrial. If only we would open our eyes and understand what we are looking at in the backgrounds…if only we could just wake up and see!

## *The Author's Personal Experiences*

### Was It a Dream?

In August 1963, I stayed overnight down along Coombs Ferry with a woman companion. She was older than me; we had met at a party. She was also more experienced in things than I was, but most of all I remember her big, friendly smile, her laughter, and freckles. She was slender, and my height, which was at 5'7" in those youthful days! We had a small fire going, and I had fixed our bedding. It was close to midnight when we finally went to sleep after an enjoyable evening. It was a quiet night, and we were far away from any other campers. I recall it was hot and muggy, and there was a mild mist that floated on the water that sometimes touched the rocky beach.

As I lay there resting, I saw that my companion was contently sleeping next to me. It was one of those gentle, fulfilling nights where a person did not have to worry about anything, really, because John F. Kennedy was President of the United States, employment was stable, AIDS and other social diseases were not a problem, and the Viet Nam War was not even thought of at that time. The summer of 1963 held many blessings for me and this night was one of them. I closed my eyelids...only to open them a few moments later because I felt and knew I was not alone at Coombs Ferry.

Watching the shoreline, there seemed to be some kind of light out in the water, which I thought might be people in a boat fishing. As it drew nearer, it seemed to pause, and the mists of the night covered it with a cloak, and for a moment or so, the light vanished. Then I saw a figure coming up from and out of the water. I felt drawn to her. This woman was tall with blonde hair that seemed to have a white cast to it in the flickering flames from the campfire. Her hair was long and she was naked, beautifully so. I could not guess or tell her age. I could not talk it seemed. I remember she knelt beside my female companion and touched her hand to the sleeper's face. There seemed an odd sort of gray cloud surrounding the campfire, the stranger, and us. I remember my companion awoke, as if in a dream, and came beside me. We undressed each other and followed the stranger into the water. The woman seemed to be talking inside my head, telepathically communicating with me. I remember nothing else.

My companion and I awoke near daybreak and made love. I remarked afterwards how pretty her long brown hair looked in the morning sunrise. We went for a swim, dressed, broke camp, and left. She said she had had a strange dream last night about a tall woman talking with her, and I told her I had had a dream like that, too. We laughed, shrugged it off, and went to a café for breakfast. We saw each other once more than she went to Kansas City, Missouri, and I did not see her again. What happened that August night in 1963? What was that spell of the water, the shoreline, and the female stranger from the depths? Who or what was this woman from the lake? Was it a dream? What was it? Neither my companion nor I had been drinking. All we had was water in canteens, so we were both sober. What happened to us? Where did we go? Could this happen to somebody else, has it happened in this lake area to others since 1963, and for what purpose? Could it happen to you?

## Lights Underwater

Towards the end of August 1963, my Uncle Willard and I camped out overnight at Coombs Ferry. It was a quiet, peaceful evening. We had been discussing druids and shamans, and he mentioned that the difference between the two was basic, based on his readings and studies: "Druids have to fabricate their reason for being whereas Shamans inherited theirs intrinsically."

A short time later, after sharing a big can of pork and beans, we both saw lights floating under the water not far from the rocky shoreline. We decided it was not divers out for a midnight swim, but something circular. These well-arranged lights seemed like running board lights. We could not make out details other than that. It never surfaced and continued on its path towards the middle of the lake, moving slowly away as if it was in search of something. What was it? This was the only time when we were together at Coombs Ferry that my Uncle Willard and I saw such an occurrence. It was the last time we spent the night there before I went to live in Santa Monica Canyon; we never found another opportunity to camp together in this area or the Missouri Ozarks. Uncle Willard died in 1979.

I would urge those with a keen interest in the paranormal and the extraterrestrial to explore Coombs Ferry by both water and land. There is something mysterious and enchanting about this area that will fascinate, charm, and intrigue you. Perhaps, you and your friends could spend a night there, wait and listen, and see what happens next! Recall that old saying: "All things come to he or she who waits!" Just what those things might be is something to consider and wonder about.

## Spirit Encounters

In late May 2009, my wife Debra and I took another journey to Branson to visit different places. We thought it would be a great idea to visit Coombs Ferry and see what changes, if any, had taken place there, but we were totally unprepared for the spirit encounters we would across!

Coombs Ferry can be found easily enough by taking Highway 65 out of Branson; following Highway 65 South, turn right at Highway 86. Turn right again onto Highway JJ that takes you on County Road JJ-80, which dead-ends further on a ways. In recent years Coombs Ferry has become a camping ground for the Army Corps of Engineers, and has a ramp to allow boats onto the water. It is as eerie now as it was when I spent many a fine time there. You will know you are on the right road if just before you reach the clearing to the boat loading ramp, you pass a well-kept, quiet-looking cemetery on the driver's side of the car; it is on the left of the paved road as you drive towards the ramp.

My wife Debra and I were in for several surprises at Coombs Ferry, and they were all connected with spirit contact. These spirit contacts were what we would identify as intelligent hauntings, and the ghosts spanned different time periods. We did not have access to what the immediate area of Coombs Ferry would have looked like over the past three hundred years or where the water levels would have been during those times.

We arrived in early afternoon. The road comes into a large clearing and there were many bags of trash and other material piled onto a centralized corner near where the road had been blocked off by brush and bulldozer pilings. To go further into the area would no longer be possible by automobile. Access would have to be by boat or wading the edge of the water to make for further exploration. Much of the area remains abandoned and is not in use. Still, the main outlet leading down to the water was intact.

I was delighted to discover the same rock area I had last camped at over thirty-five years ago. Some scrub brush and small trees had moved closer to the rocks, but otherwise, it was as it was the last time I came this way. I had not been there more than a few minutes when I felt the presence of spirits. Soon, *very soon* after arriving, I was in contact with the dead; it was a most positive experience. At one point, I was surrounded by eight children, ranging in age from five to twelve years old; three boys and five girls. I could sense their touching my clothes and forming a friendly circle around me. They ran in a slow circle around me, and I loved the sound of their young, happy laughter. Were they the same ghost children of long ago? Yes, they knew my name and called out to me. I was pleased. I told them in a gentle voice I had returned and was older now by many years, but knew them and thanked them for welcoming me back. I felt some more gentle tugging at my shirt and arms, and then as quickly as they had come, they vanished, laughing.

While this contact was taking place with me, Debra was experiencing her own contact in our automobile parked in the shade. She was sitting there watching me when the ghost of an elderly man suddenly appeared beside her in the driver's seat. The man asked her if his Lorraine was all right. Debra said she did not know. He asked the question again, and Debra repeated her answer to him in a kind manner, added this that she was sure everything was all right. As quickly as the elderly man had come, he disappeared. There was only a slight coolness in the automobile to mark his passing and a sweet scent that neither of us could identify.

Debra and I discussed what we had encountered, and we both agreed the area was filled with spirits. Coombs Ferry was an active focal point for spirit contact and, given the right circumstances, a psychic investigation team spending some nights and days camping in this area would find some amazing discoveries. I told Debra that the children seemed from different time periods; during the few seconds in which I could see them, their clothes each told a story. To put it into perspective, my analysis is that the children came from time periods covering the 1800s through the 1950s. I had succeeded in making contact with four, possibly five, of those children.

The lively ringleader of this children's group, so to speak, seemed to be a ten-year-old redheaded girl with short hair. She was dressed in clothes children wore during the 1940s; her dress was a pretty flower design in white and she wore what appeared to be white socks and brown lace-up shoes. I remember she looked at me and told me there was more to come and to be patient, please. An older boy around twelve-years-old, who was wearing similar era clothes in the manner of coveralls but was barefooted, echoed the same exact words the little girl had spoken in an excited, high-pitched voice.

Debra and I were pleased with our contact with the spirit world. It was a clear, sunny day without a breeze, as if everything had settled into a quiet dimension of nature. The temperature was pleasant in the shade, and bordered on the cool that can be expected this time of year in the Missouri Ozarks. However, walk out into the bright sunlight and you could feel the sun hitting your body and warming you quickly. The water around Coombs Ferry was glassy and smooth. At one point, when I was near the water, the children surrounded me again, but as soon as they came, they ran laughing away and vanished. It was a pleasant sensation, and I felt their affection. The children ran towards Debra and seemed startled to find her there. At first, they were hesitant, but then they ran on their way.

Some more exploration of the area found nothing, but the air was crisp with spirit activity, so Debra and I went elsewhere in this perfect spirit haven! We let the spirits guide us...but soon it was time to start back as dusk was less than an hour away. We got in the car and started back down the road. I had not gone far when I passed an open area and heard my name being called out twice. I stopped and backed up to where I had heard the voice calling my name. There was a very rough opening on the left side of the road. Actually, the paved section had worn thin and was non-existent in areas — it was a drop-off of over a foot onto the ground. I took the chance, and slowly moved the car down and off the paved road into one of the most perfect glades with tall trees whose limbs provided a canopy of protection from the overhead sun. I got out of the car, leaving it running. Debra remained inside the car.

I barely had time to close the car door when the spirit of an elderly woman touched me. Within seconds, I was surrounded by several "women" who touched me and were talking excitedly as they gently crowded up against me. I felt an instant affinity for these women, but I could not define it. I knew they were of different time eras, mostly from the past 200 years. I was amazed to hear their lively speaking, although some of it was not in English. I felt comfortable in their presence! I could not help but wonder about the area having so much wonderful psychic energy and spirit magnetism.

A sensitive feels and sees the paranormal in different ways. I could hear them, I could see them, and they had made contact with me in an intelligent manner that went past the defined confines of an intelligent haunting. They lived here — this was their home. It was a home for ghosts from the past that had migrated to Coombs Ferry. I was further amazed to know these ghosts did not want my wife and I to leave! I walked the short distance back to where Debra was watching from the car. I opened the door and shared with her what I had encountered. She said the area was full of spirits. She *felt* their presences and believed this was a migration point for ghosts from a long past that stretched back into time. I agreed.

I got inside the car and we rolled down our front windows. We told the spirits that had welcomed us to their home that we appreciated them and their allowing us to visit, and we thanked them many times for revealing themselves to us in such a clear and kind manner. We talked with these ghostly inhabitants a while longer and then it was time to leave. We thanked them again. A ghostly presence that had been sitting in our back seat vanished and joined the others. We wished them well and said goodbye. They did not want us to leave. We told them that we would return and visit them again, but it was hard to depart from this setting, for it was so peaceful and quiet. We will come back another time.

~~~~~

Coombs Ferry is definitely haunted, and it seems a strong spirit migration point. It deserves further investigation. There are many paranormal occurrences taking place in this area that both intrigue and amaze. The spirits are friendly. The ghostly hauntings are real and offer some keen insights into the world of the paranormal. Visit the area if you are near Branson, for it is well worth your time!

## *Indian Point*

Directly across from Coombs Ferry is another beautiful area named Indian Point. The lake water separates the two locations, and in some areas the water depth is over 100 feet. The water hides many things! This area of water contains many sunken boats and other incidents from the past now lost and forgotten in the mists of time.

There are stories of divers encountering oddities off Indian Point, and it is said that no diver should go alone or at night to dive the depths that lay in wait off of Indian Point. There is one story of two divers doing a night dive and one of them being punched in the stomach by an entity. There were no giant bottom-feeding catfish, no giant gars or anything of that nature, and nothing was reflected in the large beacon-like underwater light held tightly in the diver's hand. Only a fleeting presence of something surreal and not part of the natural underwater landscape was what touched him. His companion was pushed aside by the same presence. Something toyed with them briefly and then vanished in the murky depths. What was this ghostly apparition that seemed to have form but at the same time not form?

One person I visited with said he had seen lights under the water's surface once when he had been fishing and that the lights passed under his boat at a fair speed and then suddenly went off. He said the lights reminded him of circular deck lights.

Sightings of a Confederate soldier have been reported in the woods near Indian Point. The apparition is seen running through the deep woods — many deep woods locations offer cover for various things. Whether this turns out to be an intelligent or residual haunting has not been defined. It is hard to track a ghost, apparition, or spirit in heavily wooded areas unless that entity wants contact and is in close proximity to the paranormal investigator. By whatever name you call the entity you are pursuing and trying to make contact with, it may or may not select you as its contact. Do not be irritated or alarmed, because that is sometimes how it works. For instance, just as you may want to make contact with somebody in your immediate social setting, that person may not care or wish to make contact with you. Whether on a paranormal or human level of interpretative contact, that may be how it works in any given circumstance or situation for the contact and the contactee.

As noted in the Coombs Ferry section, a UFO disc is said to have exploded above the water and scattered its contents and wreckage in the body of water between Indian Point and Coombs Ferry. No known documentation of wreckage findings or rubble from the incident have been reported, or revealed, to the public. One can only wonder what may lay buried or scattered in the area.

Paranormal happenings and UFO occurrences oftentimes share the same body of water or land. Neither has a monopoly on a given area. Each encounter, whichever it happens to be, is a distinct learning experience for humans.

# Chapter Eight:

# Nebraska

Noted for its farming and ranching, Nebraska has an ongoing history of civil rights activism that started in 1912. Omaha is the largest city and Lincoln is the capital. The state has many National Park Service locations, including the Lewis & Clark Historic Trail and the Pony Express National Historic Trail.

There are many famous people connected with the state of Nebraska, including Gerald R. Ford, Mari Sandoz, Fred Astaire, Ruth Etting, Peter Fonda, Henry Fonda, Sandra Dennis, James Coburn, Lillian St. Cyr, Johnny Carson, Barbara Barnes Lucas, Swoosie Kurtz, Hilary Swank, Julie Sommars, Malcolm X, Leta Stetter Hollingsworth, Willa Cather, John G. Neihardt, Coleen Gray, David Janssen, Marg Helgenberger, Nick Nolte, Gordon MacRae, Marlon Brando, Ward Bond, Lyle Talbot, Robert Taylor, Harold G. Borland, Ernest K. Gann, and Max Baer.

Nebraska is the home of Arbor Day. This event was founded by J. Sterling Morton. A region of contrasts, the cities are usually small and very friendly.

## Blair

Dana College is located in Blair, Nebraska. This small, pleasant college was originally established by Danish settlers of the Lutheran faith in 1884. Paranormal occurrences at the college include:

† Ghost activity in different halls and buildings.
† Shadow figures roam the campus at will, appearing at no set time. Suddenly they are there!
† Music and laughter are heard, but never pinpointed. The ghostly sounds come quickly and then fade and vanish.

† Students have reported bumping into invisible forces, and people say they have been touched by invisible fingers.

† A man without a face was seen in one of the men's restrooms.

# WEEPING WATER

Settled in 1856, Weeping Water, Nebraska, became a city in 1883. It has many older buildings made of limestone, and is known for its beautiful hills and fresh, clean air.

Weeping Water has an interesting history; the Weeping Water Valley Historical Museum offers insights into the city and its early settlers.

The cemetery at Weeping Water is, reputedly, haunted. Stories of paranormal activity occurring there have been reported, including ghosts appearing in the cemetery at night and sounds of whispering.

# DORCHESTER

A haunted cemetery named Gilbert's Graveyard is located in Dorchester, Nebraska; the graveyard is named after pioneers who settled the area. The paranormal activity includes:

† Shadow figures lurking behind tombstones and other grave markings.

† A ghostly old couple is heard talking, and the voices of young children have been heard in the middle of the cemetery on nights of a full moon.

† A ghost dog is said to haunt the cemetery during the midnight hour; it barks three times and then disappears. The dog may be an intelligent haunting.

# OGALLALA

Founded in 1868, stores on its Front Street will remind visitors of Ogallala's Western heritage. Once upon a time the Pony Express stopped there, and later came railroad connections.

There are reports of hauntings in Ogallala's cemeteries. Many hauntings are said to be ghosts from the Wild West days of the town;

sightings of ghosts in cowboy clothes have been reported. The incidence of cowboy ghosts does lend itself more readily to areas in which they lived and worked, and the Midwest has its fair share of valid hauntings featuring cowboy ghosts.

Ogallala Aquifer is located in the city and is considered the world's largest underground water supply. Ogallala is known as the cowboy capitol of Nebraska. This colorful and friendly town has fifteen churches and many parks.

# CROFTON

A charming town, Crofton, Nebraska, is home to the haunted Argo Hotel. Constructed in 1911 of brick, the hotel is located at 211 Kansas Avenue. Over the decades, it had different owners and different names. In 1935, it became a medical clinic. Its interesting structure made it possible for listing on the National Register of Historic Places.

The building was renovated during the 1990s and reclaimed its original name as the Argo Hotel. The ground and second floors and basement are haunted. The bones of an infant were uncovered during restoration, and there are many accounts of paranormal activity and apparitions. Other ghost stories include:

† A haunting involving a young mother and her infant child.
† The appearance of two men on the second floor that suddenly disappear.
† The ghosts of previous patients who visited the hotel when it was a clinic and later owned by a physician have been seen.
† Whispers and footsteps have been heard in the basement.
† Both intelligent and residual hauntings by visitors who are deceased may exist here, and orbs have been seen in three of its rooms.

# FREMONT

Fremont Lakes Recreational Area in Fremont, Nebraska, was constructed over a cemetery. It is said that some of the bodies were lost over a period of time without identifying markers and, as a direct result, these bodies were not recovered and lay buried under the peaceful façade of the park.

Stories of the appearance of ghostly people is not uncommon, and they may be both intelligent and residual hauntings.

Shadow figures are often seen in the park, appearing in both the daylight and early evening. There is said to be the shadow figure of a young woman that walks the park, but, upon approach, she fades into a white mist and vanishes as quickly as she was seen!

# ALLIANCE

Alliance, Nebraska, is the home of the Alliance Theater. Originally the Charter Hotel when it opened for business in 1903, it became a movie theater during 1937–38. With its unusual design, it is considered a masterpiece of the art deco modern era, and its imaginative appearance was ahead of its time. It is located at 410 Box Butte Avenue in Alliance and continues to entertain patrons with new films.

Friendly ghosts are said to haunt the theater. There are many reports of shadow figures that approach people and then disappear a short distance away. It is as if they are curious about the living people who are walking into the theater! Other hauntings include:

† A young woman and her boyfriend are said to be part of the living audience, their ghostly appearance unnoticed except if you look closely and see they are wearing clothes from the 1940s era.

† A young girl is sometimes seen at the entrance of the theater; she seems to be looking for somebody, but upon approach she is said to vanish.

† A ghost cat with orange fur has been seen at the theater entrance and vanishes while meandering down the sidewalk.

† Ghostly laughter has been heard in the men's restroom at various times, and an elderly lady is heard talking in the women's restroom on Saturdays.

~~~~~

There is a feeling of peace in the theater, and the ghosts keep it that way!

**Chapter Nine:**

# North Dakota

With coal and oil as its economic bases, these energy items have had a continuing positive effect on the economy of North Dakota. There are American Indian tribal colleges located here, including the United Tribes Technical College in Bismarck.

Known for its Red River and Red River Valley, these areas have made agriculture a prime importance for the state. North Dakota contains plains and flatlands. The Theodore Roosevelt National Park is located in the badlands section and Devil's Lake is situated in the east.

Native Americans lived in North Dakota for over 5,000 years. They began trading with French explorers in 1738.

There are many famous people connected with the state of North Dakota, including Ann Sothern, Lawrence Welk, Peggy Lee, Sitting Bull, Louis L'Amour, Eric Sevaried, Larry Woiwode, Roger Maris, Angie Dickinson, Ivan Dmitri, Bobby Vee, Josh Duhamel, Shannon Curfman, Cynthia Jelleborg, Linda Whitney, Ric Sprynczynatyk, Leonard Peltier, and Celeste Krenz.

Internationally known in paranormal circles, Troy Parkinson lives in Fargo, North Dakota, where he continues his life work as a medium. In 2006, the Rock & Roll legend Alice Cooper was given a gold-plated key and a marble plaque when he visited the city of Alice, North Dakota, on his way to a concert performance in Fargo.

## Fargo

North Dakota State University is located in Fargo, Nebraska, and, according to different reports, haunted areas include Minard Hall, Ceres Hall, and the Administration Building. Students claim to have seen the ghosts of both women and men, and there is a story about two men locked in combat and moaning as if fighting a personal battle that never has relief, pause, or ending.

Voices without bodies have also been heard, and feelings of unrest and being ill at ease reported at different points on campus. A female student is said to be heard crying and walking the halls on campus, but she's not seen.

# AMIDON

Founded in 1910 as an agricultural town, Amidon, North Dakota, is located in Slope County near the city of White Butte. In 1920, it had a population of less than 200 people. The city was named after Judge Charles F. Amidon and is considered by many as a ghost town since its population is less than twenty-five people today. It is still the county seat and most of its buildings are empty.

The local restaurant is named "Georgia's and the Owl," and it's found on US-85 and Main Street. It is, reputedly, haunted by the ghost of a mischievous young boy that appears around people and then vanishes, laughing in their presence.

# FORT YATES

The tribal headquarters for the Standing Rock Sioux Tribe is located in Fort Yates. It has a given population of 228. The first US Army post was established here in 1863, and its name was changed in 1876 to honor Captain George Yates who was killed at the Battle of the Little Big Horn with General George A. Custer.

This area has some interesting paranormal occurrences that could involve both residual and intelligent hauntings. One such occurrence is the reputed haunting of Captain George Yates, who returns sporadically to the fort grounds to show his appreciation for the post having honored him by dedicating the fort in his name. Some say his ghost is seen walking to the north sector of the original post grounds, and he is in full military dress. He is said to walk a short distance, turn around, walk back, and then vanish. He haunts the post every fourteenth day of each month.

A group of soldiers laughing and talking is seen and heard, but upon approach, they turn and vanish. These soldiers may be from the time of the fort's inception immediately after the American Civil War. Another ghost is that of a tall, emaciated man in full military dress walking towards the fort calling to somebody or some thing; he is oblivious to those who try to hail him.

The ghost of Sitting Bull and other Native Americans are seen in the area. At one time, Sitting Bull was seen sitting in a rocking chair, and both Sitting Bull and the rocking chair vanished as quickly as they had appeared. Sitting Bull was arrested at Fort Yates December 14, 1890, and was later buried there before his body was removed. Some accounts state the body was removed and reburied in Mobridge, South Dakota.

Other ghosts include a tall older woman with auburn hair, wearing a yellow shawl and long white dress, and carrying a small brown suitcase. She has been seen at the outskirts of the fort, but disappears upon being noticed by the living. A ghost dog is said to approach people and bark once and then suddenly turn and run away, vanishing into a soft gray mist. Voices, laughter, and a man farting loudly have also been heard.

The old government jail, now used for storage, is said to contain the ghosts of former prisoners. Sounds of a man spitting chewing tobacco are heard infrequently.

## Luger Hotel

Built by Richard Luger in the 1950s, the Luger Hotel is a scene of many hauntings. Some of them may be intelligent hauntings and in need of paranormal investigation to verify what is going on. There are many reports of the basement in this old hotel being haunted, as people are wary of going down there alone for fear of being groped or touched by invisible fingers of several women ghosts. In recent years, these laughing women ghosts have been silent.

The ghosts of children are often seen on different hotel floors, and they appear to be playing and happy. There is the story of a little girl in a pink dress said to run from room to room in an unending game of touching each doorframe and then hurrying on to another one. Voices talking are often heard in different parts of the old hotel.

## *Other Haunts*

† Standing Rock High School is said to be haunted. One of the ghosts is a young male student who died there.

† Not far from Fort Yates is the mysterious location identified as Black Tongue Hill — an old woman who lived in that area haunts it. The ghost is an elderly woman wearing a pretty black dress with red embroidered roses around the neck of the garment. A victim of an unknown hit and run driver, now she is frequently seen on the road looking for the car or truck containing the driver who killed her.

~~~~~

An important aspect of both military fort and hotel locations in the same immediate area is that they sometimes seem to attract ghosts and reflect ghostly hauntings and paranormal occurrences. There is much in the way of paranormal activity awaiting those who wish to investigate old military forts and hotels. These two locations are often like magnets to ghosts! They are there…waiting.

# DICKINSON

Sounds of children at play at different places are heard at St. Joseph's Hospital in Dickinson, North Dakota, though the children are never seen. Shadow figures have been seen lurking in the halls, and a shrill whistle being blown is sometimes heard near the administrative offices. No explanation as to why it is heard or where it comes from has been given.

# ABERCROMBIE

This lively setting for ghosts includes the Fort Abercrombie area, which is said to be filled with the ghosts of soldiers and American Indians. Stories of seeing such ghosts are not unusual. Photographs of the ghosts in action has been attempted, but without success.

The solitary figure of an American Indian sitting on top of his horse has been seen often in and around the city. The ghosts appear to be all residual hauntings from the past of the American West.

# MANDAN

Founded in 1879, Mandan, North Dakota, became the county seat in 1881. Located near the city of Bismarck, Mandan's slogan is "Where the West Begins."

An important location during the settlement of the west, Fort Abraham Lincoln State Park is within seven miles of Mandan. Historically, the Mandan Tribe established its first Native American village there in 1575. On-A-Slant Indian Village was a major settlement for the Mandan Tribe from 1575–1781. The location is near where the Missouri River comes together with the Heart River. White Coyote, a Mandan chief who guided the Lewis & Clark Expedition, was born at the Mandan settlement in 1766.

Custer House, where George Armstrong Custer and his wife Libby lived, is at the fort location and, although it burned down in 1874, it was rebuilt. The fort also had a barracks that held room for nine companies, a hospital, and other amenities. Custer was the first post commander from 1873 until his death at the Battle of Little Big Horn in 1876. The fort was established June 14, 1872.

As a note of interest, the original fort was abandoned and its wood and nails used by local residents for construction of their own homes and other city structures. This was not an uncommon practice among the early settlers. A new fort was rebuilt across the river from the old location in 1885.

As to hauntings and paranormal occurrences, this entire area has them. There are stories of the widowed wives of the Custer disaster bemoaning the lost of their dead husbands killed in the decisive victory for the Indians at the Battle of Little Big Horn. These tormented ghosts are said to moan and cry… Their voices are heard in the winds that permeate the area of the fort and the Custer House, and sometimes can even be heard on the wind coming across the river. There is a story of a man who committed suicide at the fort and whose lonely ghost now haunts it.

The ghost of White Coyote, reportedly, haunts the old encampment site of Lewis & Clark, and the Mandan Indians are often seen in the hills near the river. An image of Lewis & Clark and their group have been said to appear near where the rivers come together in the winter months when there's snow.

## Libby Custer

The ghost of Libby Custer has been seen sitting inside her house in a rocking chair, her eyes fixed on a sight outside the window, perhaps sensing that her husband has just died — her ghost vanishes upon approach. Another sighting of Libby Custer is of her standing on the front porch of the Custer home, seemingly watching for somebody or patiently waiting. This ghost disappears upon approach, but not before it stares back at you in surprise!

Libby Custer did not remarry after the death of her husband, and she did much to keep his memory alive and untarnished while she was alive. She wrote the best-selling book *Boots and Saddles* (1885), among other writings, and gave popular lectures that were well-attended. The love story of Libby and George Custer is in itself an interesting saga found in the stories of Western marriages during the aftermath of the American Civil War. Custer is recognized as a military hero for his uncompromising bravery during American Civil War battles.

That George Custer and Libby were a devoted couple has been well-documented, and their intimate love story is well-known in fiction and history writings. History also reveals Custer as a chance-taker, as some of his most amazing battle participations during the American Civil War resulted from his acute intuition to seize the day and attack. Over the decades, there is the story told that Custer sensed his impeding death at the Battle of the Little Big Horn and communicated it in personal ways to Libby. One story has it that an elderly American Indian ghost visited Custer shortly before his leaving for Little Big Horn and told him if he went there he would die. Much legend, myth, and paranormal material surrounds Custer's premonition of death in battle during the engagement with the Indians at the Battle of Little Big Horn.

One rumor says that had Custer not been killed in the battle, he would have run against President Grant and probably would have been elected President of the United States. It has been suggested that President Ulysses S. Grant (1822–1885) gave a loud sigh of relief when he was told Custer had died, and much information has surfaced in recent times about the jealousy Grant held for the charming, brash Custer. The burial site for Custer is in the post cemetery at the United States Military Academy at West Point in New York. His wife, Libby, is buried with him. They never had any children. Libby died April 6, 1933, in New York.

There have been stories of the ghosts of George and Libby Custer being seen near the river, the fort, and the house they lived in; each story varies depending upon how it is told and by whom.

~~~~~

Stories of military men at the old fort site have also been told, and some ghost stories involve sounds, singing, and visual sightings. The American West and the American Civil War dominate to some degree the imagination of most Americans — and their ghosts are still very much with us!

# MEDORA

A peaceful town with a colorful history and a friendly atmosphere, Medora, North Dakota, was founded by a young French aristocrat named Marquis de Mores (1858–1896). Mores named the town after his wife, whose name was Medora. He built many of the city structures, including the hotel and St. Mary's Catholic Church. "Medora Musical" is one of the major tourist attractions in the state. The town has excellent eating establishments.

Marquis de Mores' summer home and hunting lodge were donated to the state of North Dakota in 1936 and fully restored as a museum by 1941. Now named the Chateau de Mores Historical Site, this two-story, 26-room structure includes 128 acres.

The chateau is, reputedly, haunted by the ghost of Marquis de Mores, who frequents the rooms. Sounds of whispering are heard in several rooms on both the upper and lower floors. Orbs have been seen in rooms on the second floor, and the sound of a woman softly singing has been heard in two different rooms on the first floor.

## *Other Haunts*

† Theodore Roosevelt hunted buffalo in the area in 1883 — and his ghost is said to still haunt the area. Tourists and visitors have reported seeing his ghost.
† Shadow figures have been seen at the Fudge Depot.
† Friendly ghosts of young children, reportedly, haunt the Rough Rider Hotel.

# Chapter Ten:
# SOUTH DAKOTA

The Mount Rushmore State, in 2010 South Dakota was ranked the forty-sixth state in population with less than 900,000 people. Its capital is located at Pierre, and its largest city is Sioux Falls. Known for its agricultural economy and pleasant rural lifestyle, hunting and fishing are popular for the state's residents and influx of tourists. In addition to agriculture, retail, banking, finance, and health care dominate the economic system. The famous Black Hills are in South Dakota. The state is a grasslands setting and it was here that sculptor Gutzon Borglum created his famous Mount Rushmore figures of four United States Presidents. It is referred to today as the Mount Rushmore National Memorial.

The first inhabitants were hunters who came to the state over 5,000 years ago or longer. An extensive cave system is found at Wind Cave National Park. Deadwood is South Dakota's most famous gold town. It has taken on a mythic standing in the legends of the American West.

There are many famous people connected with the state of South Dakota, including Ernest O. Lawrence, Cheryl Ladd, Myron Floren, L. Frank Baum, JoAnne Bird, Jess Thomas, Mamie Van Doren, Tom Brokaw, Red Cloud, Oscar Howe, George McGovern, Allison Hedge Coke, Gertrude Bonnin, Elizabeth Cook-Lynn, Joseph Hansen, Jess Thomas, Floyd "Red Crow" Westerman, Crazy Horse, Rain-in-the-Face, and Cameron Hawley.

## GREGORY

Founded in 1904, Gregory, South Dakota, is a town with a lot of history — *and hauntings*. It's also home to many old buildings, and two areas of reputed paranormal occurrences are the Hipp Theater and Oscar Micheaux Center. A trip down Main Street is an enjoyable walk through the past in this western town.

Oscar Micheaux (1884–1951) was the first black homesteader in Gregory, and his contributions in movie making and writing put him at the top of early African-American people to achieve important recognition for their contributions to American culture. His ghost has been seen at the Oscar Micheaux Center.

The Hipp Theater has ghosts and shadow figures. Sounds of laughter without a body to accompany it have been noted in the women's restroom while sounds of footsteps without the presence of feet to accompany them have been heard in the men's restroom. This pleasant movie theater shows first-run features and has a comfortable atmosphere about it. Looking at the concession area and the lobby, one wonders about the many ghosts that still enjoy mingling about with the living!

# FIRESTEEL

One location that appears frequently in stories by ghost hunters is Firesteel, South Dakota. According to state highway map directions, it is now is listed as a village with a population of sixty-five people. It can be reached by going northwest of Pierre on Highway 20.

Sadly, Firesteel derives its ghosts and paranormal status from a mine disaster. Different accounts of the tragedy are available, but essentially the story is it was a coal mining disaster in 1934 that resulted in the deaths of eighty-nine miners. Firesteel is said to be haunted by an abundance of shadow figures throughout the city, and the voices of ghostly miners are frequently heard in the city and around the mines. These ghosts have also been seen walking in the city.

At this point in time, further documentation by paranormal groups is needed to verify these intelligent and residual hauntings, and the other paranormal occurrences taking place in this village, which was once a thriving place before World War II.

Mine disasters loom large in paranormal occurrences, and the ghosts found connected with such disasters are prevalent throughout recorded history. There is something about such happenings that intrigue the public at-large, and where there is an old abandoned mine, there is most likely a ghost tale or two or three to accompany it. As long as there are mine disasters, abandoned mines, or sealed-off mines, the presence of ghosts will remain and Firesteel, South Dakota, is one such location!

# WOUNDED KNEE

One of America's most horrible incidents occurred at Wounded Knee, South Dakota. On December 29, 1890, the infamous Wounded Knee massacre took place at the Pine Ridge Indian Reservation where over 300 Sioux, many of them women and children, were slaughtered in a bloodletting frenzy by American troops. Scrotums, breasts, and other fleshy parts were sliced off the Indian victims as souvenirs to be made into tobacco pouches, good luck charms, and coin purses. It has been documented that a large percentage of the Indian victims were mutilated while still alive and left to freeze to death in the harsh winter weather.

This location was once again the scene for unrest on February 27, 1973, when the American Indian Movement occupied the Pine Ridge Reservation in protest against federal government policies directed at American Indians and the Pine Ridge Reservation. This occupation lasted seventy-one days and captured world attention for the cause of American Indians.

A third situation occurred in 1975 involving a shootout on the Pine Indian Reservation; two Federal Bureau of Investigations agents were killed. Leonard Peltier, a member of the American Indian Movement and a key activist, was sentenced to two life imprisonments for killing the two FBI agents.

Leonard Peltier has remained a controversial figure since his imprisonment. Peter Matthiessen, in his documented account of how the FBI waged war on the American Indian Movement and framed Leonard Peltier for the two FBI agent killings, compiled the known facts into a best-selling non-fiction book titled *In the Spirit of Crazy Horse* (1983) and Michael Apted's popular DVD documentary, "Incident at Oglala: The Leonard Peltier Story," was released worldwide in 1992. There has been a tremendous amount of material written about Leonard Peltier since 1975, and part of the urban legends surrounding this writer/artist is the on-going suggestion that no American President will ever pardon Peltier for fear the FBI will have that President assassinated!

Recent investigations by the General Accounting Offices Fraud Division accuse the US Federal Government of misusing legally appropriated monies by the US Federal Government for legitimate Indian Causes. The report cites in specifics that over the past fifty years the Bureau of Indian Affairs has misplaced and lost track of three billion dollars designated to help American Indians. The legal questions being asked the US Federal Government is how it misplaced such a huge sum of money, where did it really go, and who really got hold of it. The General Accounting Offices Fraud Division wants to know — and so does America!

As a place for hauntings, this area has them. The mutilated ghosts of the American Indians are said to wander the area where they died December 29, 1890. Also, ghost children are oftentimes seen running and screaming in pain in the Pine Indian Reservation setting. The ghost of a young mother beheaded by a soldier's saber is seen walking with her young daughter — they are looking for the mother's head.

Other ghostly tales have come down through time since 1890, including more recent ones. One story involves the ghosts of the two FBI agents in their car pursing their quarry and vanishing over a hill. Am attractive Indian woman in her thirties wearing black jeans, black shirt, black boots, and a black jacket is seen at different locations, and she is said to be looking for somebody. She does not linger, but appears momentarily and then disappears. There have been stories told over the decades of people having seen the ghosts of young children walking alongside roads — these children are suddenly there one instant and gone the next! There is much paranormal activity in this area before and since 1890 that requires further paranormal investigation and documentation.

Generally, in any situation where acts of violence have taken place, there is much residue left behind. There are residual hauntings. There are intelligent hauntings. The sounds of the dying are registered in the ethers of time, and so are their ghosts. It is up to paranormal investigators to seek them out or, better yet, have them seek out the paranormal investigators so their stories can be known.

Paranormal investigators discover something new every time a new setting is come upon, and even though that same setting may have been previously investigated before, there is still the chance something else may be there waiting to be unveiled and fully revealed. The living knows less at times than they think they do when it comes to paranormal occurrences.

I have heard many ghost hunters say that an intelligent haunting is capable of change and delivery. Well, if it is truly an intelligent haunting, then that is a logical explanation. Whereas residual hauntings are locked into time and space and simply repeat themselves, then it is expected those ghost images will be there again and again to revisit. This opens up a whole new avenue of debate, discussion, and thought concerning the role(s) of an intelligent haunting. There is much to be learned from the dead. Paranormal occurrences are never boring! Neither are ghosts! We learn as we go along, and it is an evolving process of learning to understand the ghosts of the dead and come to terms with what they may want.

# CHEYENNE RIVER

Near the forks of the river was the birthplace of American Indian leader, Rain-in-the-Face (1835–1905), at Cheyenne River, South Dakota. He was a war chief of the Lakota Tribe. His acts of bravery in battle made him a legendary figure among American Indians, and he was highly respected as a warrior. He was among the leaders who defeated General George Armstrong Custer at the Battle of Little Big Horn during June 25-26, 1876. The American Indian name for this famous battle with Custer is the Battle of Greasy Creek. The commanders of the battle were Sitting Bull, Crazy Horse, and Chief Gall.

Rain-in-the-Face's ghost is said to ride a pale horse in the Cheyenne River area running through South Dakota, and he has been known to stop and visit with people by way of a smile before going on his way. He and his horse are said to go a short distance and then slowly fade and disappear. Rain-in-the-Face is described as an older man wearing full Lakota wardress and carrying a long spear with the blade point facing skyward. This could be an intelligent haunting.

# YANKTON

Mount Mary College is located in Yankton, South Dakota. Situated on the bluffs of the Missouri River, it is a private college established in 1936 by the Sisters of Saint Benedict. This lovely college setting is home to several hauntings and paranormal occurrences, including unidentified voices and loud footsteps.

There are four known ghosts on the campus, and shadow figures have been seen in the performing arts auditorium and in the student center. On clear moonlight nights, the sound of women talking and laughing together is heard in the vicinity of the college's chapel.

# HOWARD

Howard, South Dakota, is the birthplace of American novelist Cameron Hawley, whose most remembered novel is *Executive Suite* (1952). His other popular novels include *Cash McCall* (1955), *The Lincoln Lords* (1960), and *The Hurricane Years* (1968).

Hawley was born September 19, 1905, and died February 9, 1969. His ghost is said to walk the streets of his hometown, where he is seen as an older man. He is said to be carrying a copy of his most famous novel, *Executive Suite*, and wearing a gray suit with matching gray tie, and black lace-up shoes.

# ABERDEEN

Northern State University is located at Aberdeen, South Dakota and it has a long history of hauntings and paranormal occurrences. They include:

† Students being touched by invisible entities
† Sounds of whispers at different locations on the campus.
† A west wind that comes to the campus in the summer months and, with this wind, comes eerie voices of males and females talking together. Nobody seems to know why this strange wind comes, but the wind's passage is generally short-lived.

~~~~~

Winds that carry voices or crying are not that unusual — there are many such stories given about winds throughout history and throughout the world. Nobody knows what the origin of such paranormal winds is… only that they occur, exist in time and place, and have their own agendas. Winds carrying paranormal verbal messages are part of many cultures.

# Deadwood

There have been many hauntings and paranormal occurrences at Deadwood, South Dakota. Some of the locations include Mount Mariah, Deadwood Cemetery, and Bullock Hotel. Of these three particular places, each is known to have shadow figures.

Bullock Hotel is reputed to be haunted by its original owner, and sightings of walking ghosts that vanish upon approach is also part of the hauntings found at Deadwood.

# Chapter Eleven:

# OHIO

**Buckeye State**

Ohio is known as the Buckeye State for its abundance of buckeye trees. Columbus is the capital and the most populated city, followed by Cleveland, Cincinnati, Toledo, and Dayton. The state has had more than two hundred recorded earthquakes since the year 1776!

Early people to the area were there over 13,000 years ago, and these early Native Americans left many important archeological artifacts and village mounds.

Over the years, Ohio has been home to major league teams such as the Akron Pros, Cleveland Rockers, and Cincinnati Red Stockings. Ohio's state fossil is the Trilobite genus Isotelus, and the state insect is the ladybug.

There are many famous people connected with the state of Ohio, including Tecumseh, Alice Schille, Cy Young, Bob Hope, Jim Jarmusch, Dean Martin, Alice Cary, Pontiac, Judith Resnik, Tarhe, Clark Gable, Neil A. Armstrong, Annie Oakley, Little Turtle, Zane Grey, Tyrone Power, Roy Rogers, Halle Berry, John Glenn, Louis Bromfield, Hart Crane, Ruby Dee, Wes Craven, Ambrose Bierce, Sherwood Anderson, Ulysses S. Grant, Harriet Beecher Stowe, Art Tatum, Rachel Sweet, Emma Bomeck, Gloria Steinem, Steven Spielberg, Orville Wright, Wilbur Wright, James Thurber, and William "Hopalong" Cassidy.

# LUCAS

Lucas, Ohio, is the location of Malabar State Farm Park at 4050 Bromfield Road. It was the home of beloved American writer Louis Bromfield from 1939 until the time of his death in 1956. Born in Mansfield, Ohio, December 27, 1896, he became one of the most popular writers in the United States at the publication of his first novel, *The Green Bay Tree* (1924). He wrote a total of thirty novels, many of which were made into successful movies. His travels in India are reflected in the fine novel, *The Rains Came* (1937), and other popular books include the classic *Early Autumn* (1926), for which he won the prestigious Pulitzer Prize; *Twenty-Four Hours* (1930); *The Farm* (1933); *Wild is the River* (1941); *Mrs. Parkington* (1943); and a best-selling autobiography titled *From My Experiences* (1955).

Bromfield married Mary Appleton Wood and they had three daughters. His later years were spent writing about nature, conservation, and agriculture, and his home named Malabar Farm became the physical expression of his conservation beliefs. There have been reports of the ghost of Louis Bromfield seen at Malabar State Farm Park, mingling with visitors. Sometimes he is seen as a robust man in his middle thirties and at other times as he looked near the time of his death.

The strong likelihood of either a residual haunting or an intelligent haunting could apply to the ghost of Louis Bromfield at this location. Louis Bromfield spent many happy years at Malabar and there is a sense of peace and calmness in the area, which many tourists have commented on. That a ghost returns to a peaceful setting to visit is a kind of haunting that does occur frequently.

Given Louis Bromfield's love of nature and his deep love for Malabar, his presence could be a genuine intelligent haunting. Further documentation is needed, and at this time, no photo of the Louis Bromfield ghost has been taken.

# COLUMBUS

Founded in 1812, Columbus became the state capital in 1816. As a city, Columbus is said to be heavily haunted with an abundance of paranormal occurrences dating back into the 1800s. Mirror Lake is reputed to be haunted, as is the area around Mound Street with the ghosts of early Native Americans.

## Greenlawn Cemetery

This old cemetery contains several hauntings. One haunting is of a young man wearing 1950s era clothes seen silently whistling as he looks down on a grave marker in the south section of the cemetery. Another haunting is of two young women, also in 50s era clothes, walking through the cemetery silently talking. Upon approach, they vanish. Orbs have been seen, as have shadow figures during the early evening hours.

## The Air and Space Museum

This museum is reputedly haunted by ghosts of pilots who once flew older airplanes — and they are known to become noisy.

## Children's Hospital

Built over an old abandoned graveyard is the Children's Hospital, which has multiple hauntings. However, the hauntings are random and there may be intelligent activity behind them.

## Camp Chase Confederate Cemetery

A Lady in Gray is said to haunt this cemetery where American Civil War soldiers are interred. She is described as being dressed in American Civil War era clothes, and some people have heard her weeping. Whether this ghostly lady is an intelligent haunting or not remains for ghost investigators to validate when they undertake a full search for the ghost's presence.

There are many stories of hauntings at cemeteries and graveyards containing the remains of American Civil War soldiers that are intelligent hauntings — and these hauntings make for interesting study and investigation. I have visited such cemeteries over the years, and each one does have a story to share with their human visitors. There is nothing to be alarmed at when you encounter a ghost or paranormal situation in such a setting, and chances are over time you will come upon an intelligent haunting!

If and when you do, see what this American Civil War ghost is trying to communicate and why. If communication is made or established in some manner, document what is said to you and ask questions of the ghost if possible! Should it be a residual haunting, enjoy what you witness and move on to other hauntings. As long as there are humans, there will always be ghosts somewhere wanting and waiting to communicate with them.

# ALLIANCE

Alliance, Ohio, is the mysterious setting for what was once upon a time referred to as The Old Orphanage. This structure was destroyed by fire in 2002. According to legend, orphans were buried in the basement and brutal measures were often used to instill discipline. It was reputed to have the ghost of a male worker who patrolled the premises and carried a long wooden nightstick; his ghost would vanish upon approach. The ghosts of the children buried in the basement are said to rise at each full moon and walk the immediate area of where the orphanage once stood.

Reports of screams and crying are still heard in the area where The Old Orphanage held sway over the lives of the children entrusted there. Orphanages often carry tales of mischief, abuse, beatings, sadistic treatment, mutilations, murders, untimely and unexplained deaths, and other mysterious stories that survive long after the structures are gone and the locations forgotten. The ghosts, though, *remember* how their living self was treated and will haunt a place whether or not it is still standing, in ruins, or has been destroyed. These orphanage settings are found throughout ghost investigating reports and in all places; that such abuses did exist in these places is a shameful fact found throughout the United States, and for the most part, the world.

Changes in orphanages did not really take place until after World War II. This also applies to mental asylums and the horrors that took place inside their dark settings! Any stories of abuse coming out of such places before the 1950s were often true, though not proven. Sterilizations and castrations were carried out in some of these settings on a regular basis as late as 1960. Castration was seen as having the effect of making the inmate docile and more manageable — that such a routine practice did exist in the United States and elsewhere in the world is shameful and sad. However, this practice was not limited to such social settings as orphanages and mental asylums. There are many documented reports that in rural areas where a male child was perceived as not right in the head or a potential threat to those around him, he was castrated at home in oftentimes crude and horrifying ways. The use of castration as a social method for control of males has a long history, with much written about this cruel punishment and the excuses used for doing it.

## BRADFORD

Bradford, Ohio, is where the Bradford Sanitarium was built in 1928 and then burned down in 1935. In the vicinity of where the sanitarium once stood, there is said to be shadow figures. Orbs have been seen during the early evening hours, a white, misty cloud has been seen in the area, and the sound of a woman crying heard.

## ATHENS

The Ohio University is located in Athens, Ohio, and it is said to have many hauntings. Native Americans are, reportedly, buried on campus grounds, adding to the paranormal occurrences. Hauntings in different buildings have been reported and the presence of shadow figures is prevalent.

## AKRON

A large cemetery named Rose Hill Burial Park is located in Akron — and its buried guests, reputedly, cause shadow figures, orbs, and ongoing hauntings to occur!

# CAMBRIDGE

An unusual cemetery named Northwood Cemetery is located in Cambridge and it is said to be haunted by various ghosts. Some of these ghosts are children while others are adults. A tall man wearing a 1940s era suit and hat, and carrying a long umbrella, is sometimes seen on weekends searching for something. Upon approach, this man suddenly vanishes.

Orbs have been seen at the cemetery during the night hours. One story tells of an elderly woman ghost singing, but only her lips move — there is no sound. She only appears in the south section of the cemetery on weekends and is seen infrequently.

# ASHTABULA

Chestnut Grove Cemetery is located in Ashtabula. The cemetery has a history of hauntings and shadow figures. In 1876, a Pacific Express train was crossing a bridge in the area when the bridge collapsed. Ninety people died — and now the ghosts of these ninety people are said to haunt the area. Orbs are often seen in the cemetery, as is the ghost of a little boy running through the cemetery.

# CINCINNATI

A favorite "haunt" of ghosts and ghost hunters alike, Cincinnati has a wide range of ghosts at different locations. Every cemetery has some prevailing story of a ghost being seen and vanishing, and every cemetery is said to have orbs of various colors. A colorful city with a colorful history, some of its many colorful hauntings are as follows:

† The Cincinnati Museum of Art is haunted by the misplaced ghost of an Egyptian mummy.
† Schrader Road Tunnel is haunted by murder and suicide victims who perished there.
† Buffalo Ridge contains a ghost of a headless woman in search of her head and the ghosts of an old man and a young boy laughing together.

† The Cincinnati Job Corps Center is where the ghost of a nun is said to haunt the floors.
† The Cincinnati Subway is haunted by several workers who were killed during the construction of its tunnels.

# BATAVIA

Batavia, Ohio, has its own Hell's Church, which has become a legend with the passage of time. Although Hell's Church no longer exists, there remains an old chimney that was part of it and this chimney is still intact and standing.

There are many stories about this church, most of them involving unholy rituals and vices being performed there. It would make for an interesting movie if all the stories about it not only turned out to be true, but also if the dead haunting the area truly exist!

One of the more interesting topics of ghost and paranormal investigations is the abundance of such churches with the taint of hell or horror about them! Some no longer exist, some remain in shattered or scattered ruins, and others sit abandoned. Usually with the passage of time, these church structures deteriorate and fall into ruin, subject to teenage dares and vandalism, and souvenir hunters!

I have come across individuals who collect artifacts and souvenirs from these old abandoned churches, and I recall visiting with a man who had salvaged two spindle-back chairs from a church that was said to have been involved in unholy rituals. He claimed that he could put a red candle in a circle, place the two restored chairs inside the circle, light the candle, and within a few moments these two chairs would move on their own within the circle. The chairs stopped moving when the red candle was extinguished.

Another story involving a small, upright piano from a cursed church was told to me, and the woman who rescued this oak piano from its position under a collapsed church roof swore that the piano played by itself when nobody was in the room with it! I have also been told tales involving salvaged podiums from devil churches — and each podium had a defined connection with some ghost that appeared at the podium and then vanished. One such tale involved the ghost of a woman in white with black hair who appeared at the podium, raised her fist with an angry expression on her face, and then vanished as suddenly as she had come; she came to this particular church podium and haunted it with her presence each night of the full moon.

In the course of paranormal investigations, you will come upon many people who openly discuss their church souvenirs, though some do not discuss their finds because they fear ridicule. I was told once by an older couple that they had found an old song hymnal in a church and when they touched it they immediately felt another hand place itself upon their own! According to this couple, they kept the song hymnal locked in a metal box so nobody would accidently touch it or handle it! I have been shown many such souvenirs from churches, though not all of these churches had a reputation of being evil. Some church items were left behind by accident and when the church was sold to another congregation, these objects were rediscovered.

In 1995, I discovered a lovely silver platter near the ruins of an old church in New Mexico, which I found pleasant to the touch. I later donated it to a church garage sale trying to raise money for a new wing on the house; it sold quickly. If you look carefully, you will see such religious objects often turn up at flea markets or garage sales. You never know what such an object possesses until you touch and examine it!

However, do be careful what you pick up, because there really is evil or negative energy out there. A good old-fashioned banishing ritual of a positive nature or a heartfelt personal cleansing prayer is always good to have on hand and say over any object you discover. Further, if what you do pick up feels evil or puts you ill at ease, simply drop it where you found it!

## Chapter Twelve:
# WISCONSIN

Known as a tourist friendly state, the capital of Wisconsin is Madison. Frenchman Jean Nicolet explored the region in 1634 and founded the Green Bay Colony.

Dairy farming, agriculture, lumbering, mining, manufacturing, and health care serve to make the state strong economically. Today the state has a highly diversified economy with tourism now a major industry.

During the American Civil War, the state was pro-Union. Wisconsin's politics remain part of its intricate cultural history and make for lively reading.

There are many famous people connected with the state of Wisconsin, including Liberace, Georgia O'Keeffe, Frederick March, Gena Rowlands, August Derleth, Carrie Catt, Orson Welles, Spencer Tracy, Laura Ingalls Wilder, Harry Houdini, John Muir, Don Ameche, Frank Lloyd Wright, William Defoe, Woody Herman, Bob LaFollette, Charles and John Ringling, and Jeanne Dixon.

## WAUSAU

Wausau, Wisconsin, has a most unusual movie theater named the Fillmor. At one time in its checkered history, it served as the location of a popular funeral home. It spent its later years as Roger's Cinema. The Fillmor is said to be haunted by ghosts from the former funeral home. There are two women ghosts that may or may not have died there in its basement, and there have been reports of people being touched by invisible hands.

# MARSHFIELD

A peculiar building known as Wood County Hospital Farm is located in Marshfield. This is the site of numerous ghost hauntings — hauntings that have a long history of scaring people every chance they get!

St. Joseph's Hospital is another hospital setting that carries within its halls many ghosts roaming the building. Some of these ghosts are carryovers from a different era, and when certain sections of the hospital were rebuilt, they came, too. Shadow figures are not uncommon, and visitors often hear whisperings.

It is interesting to note that many paranormal occurrences and hauntings in hospitals do involve intelligent attempts at communication between the living and the dead. People die in hospitals — that is a given fact; some do not cross over, but rather remain in the hospital where they died for one reason or another. It is up to the paranormal investigators to show respect and genuine feeling when encounters with such apparitions occur. In some interesting cases, the investigator, perhaps with the help of a medium, has helped such ghosts crossover.

## FOND DU LAC

Fond du Lac, Wisconsin, takes its name from the French, and it translates as "bottom of the lake." It has four cemeteries with paranormal activity, including orbs and shadow figures. These cemeteries include St. Charles Catholic Cemetery, Estabrooks Cemetery, Rienzi Cemetery, and Calvary Cemetery.

# BELGIUM

Belgium is near one of the most unusual shipwreck sites in the state of Wisconsin. Located in Ozaukee County, the village of Belgium is one of the most pleasant places a visitor could hope to come across while traveling this area. Harrington Beach State Park is close to the village of Belgium and less than one mile offshore is the submerged remains of the luxury steamboat named the *Niagara*. This was one of the most famous of the palace steamboats constructed, and it quickly developed a reputation as being the epitome of beauty and luxury. Launched for use in 1846, its popularity grew rapidly. Approximately 245 feet in length, it was a two-wheeled, side-wheel steamboat. A fire resulted in its sinking and there was a loss of sixty lives. Most of these deaths resulted from drowning.

Today, a mooring buoy marks the site of the shipwreck in less than fifty-three feet of water. The actual wreckage covers a distance of one-quarter mile from shore, spread out across a rocky bottom. On days when the weather and currents are good, the submerged wreck is visible from the water surface. Precisely, for divers, the *Niagara* is less than one mile from shore.

At one time, the *Niagara* had two thirty-foot paddlewheels intact. The *Niagara* sank September 24, 1856 on its voyage to Sheboygan, Wisconsin. Captain Fred S. Miller was at the ship's helm and he saved many lives. Although a reason for the quick-spreading fire that led to the quick sinking of the luxury steamboat was never determined, it was rumored that arson was involved.

For those interested in the history of the *Niagara*, an excellent article about it was published in the *Wisconsin Magazine of History* in 1999, "The History and Archaeology of the Great Lakes Steamboat Niagara," written by John Jensen. The State of Wisconsin now owns and protects the site.

When the steamboat went down, over a hundred years passed while it lay submerged and quietly resting in its shallow watery grave. With the dawn of scuba diving equipment, this suddenly changed and from the late 1950s through the 1980s open looting of the ship's remains went uncontrolled. There are many stories of how crates of precious

China, cultural artifacts, and other items were taken from the wreck and sold throughout the Midwest and elsewhere. This continued for many years, and the shipwreck received much damage by divers trying to open up areas that still contained valuable items. Even now, fragments of once expensive China dishes lie scattered about the wreck in disarray.

There are also ghost stories surrounding the sinking of the *Niagara*. There is a story about an overturned lifeboat and its passengers screaming as they drowned, and it is reputed that this scene can be witnessed on the anniversary of the steamboat's sinking during the daylight hours, much in the manner of a holographic scene superimposed upon the water's surface! A body of a woman wearing a blue dress of her era is seen spread-eagled on the shore, and a man is sitting beside her lifeless form; the man is in torment and crying hysterically. Upon approach, the man looks up, covers the woman's face with his hand, and the young couple vanish. Another version of this story suggests the couple is not young, but middle-aged. Another story is about a scattered, small group of men and women coming ashore, and as they walk onto the shore, they vanish…one following the other into nothingness. It is like an invisible portal opens and simply allows them to walk into another dimension, and then closes behind them as the last person vanishes behind the others! Is this a residual haunting, or is it what happened during some odd time slip between dimensions, or what exactly is happening to these eight people? Are time slips involved? There is much to consider, and with the passage of time and more precise understanding of time slips and related portals, perhaps an accurate answer can be found.

The *Niagara* sinking has mysterious happenings attached to it during its final voyage, and possibly some of the passengers on the steamboat as well. There is much to wonder about whom and what was involved in this maritime incident that claimed sixty lives! Over the years, there have been many paranormal theories advanced concerning time travelers from the future examining such disasters in person. It is possible to say that perhaps some of these time travelers from another future or alternate time line contributed to the actual disaster and may even die in such an occurrence. What do you think?

# BELOIT

Beloit, Wisconsin, has been called one of the most typical examples of a typical American city. It has the Logan Museum of Anthropology, Wright Museum of Art, Beloit Janesville Symphony, and a history dating back before 1800. Long a resident of the area is the Winnebago Tribe, and the first known settler to make his home near them was the French trapper and explorer Joseph Thiebault in the early 1820s.

Beloit was founded as a city in 1836 and designated an official Wisconsin city by the state on March 31, 1856. There are many notable people from the city, including geologist Thomas Chrowder Chamberlin, Tracy Silverman, Betty Everett, and Ray Chapman Andrews.

Beloit College is a popular liberal arts college internationally known for its numerous prehistoric Indian mounds on campus. Some of the activities in the city are the Beloit Heritage Days, Winterfest, Beloit International Film Festival, and the Rock & Roll Beloit Riverfest. One of landmarks is the famous Beloit Water Tower constructed in 1889, which is made of stone and is octagon-shaped. It has a height of 100 feet and originally held 100,000 gallons of water in its cypress wood tank.

Beloit has paranormal occurrences and many hauntings at different locations. American Indian ghosts have been seen at the prehistoric Indian mounds, and also in areas known to have once been inhabited by the Winnebago Tribe. The ghost of French trapper Joseph Thiebault is reputed to have been seen in the woods outside the city and downtown near local government buildings.

Beloit Turner School and the McNeel Middle School are also known to have paranormal activity. These hauntings include apparitions, sounds, and shadow figures. Another place reputed to be haunted with strange sounds and appearances is named The Manor. Various stories about the Trestles on Riverside have been told, and these stories claim repeated ghost sightings including a black man singing in the shadows.

The Hormel Plant and the Frito-Lay Plant are located in the city. Beloit is the home of the invention known today as the speedometer!

Beloit has a reputation for good restaurants, friendly people, and a general atmosphere of good will and pleasantness toward newcomers, though the city and its surrounding area may have intelligent hauntings yet to be investigated fully.

# Appleton

Harry Houdini lived in Appleton, Wisconsin, as a child on, aptly enough, Appleton Street. There are stories of him haunting his old childhood neighborhood — not as a child, but as an adult.

Houdini was best known as the world's greatest escape artist; no straightjacket, jail, handcuffs, or chains could hold him! Among his most famous stage acts was the Chinese Water Torture Cell. He made his first movie in 1901, and among his films were "The Man From Beyond," "Haldane of the Secret Service," "The Grim Game," and "Terror Island."

An injury resulting in peritonitis caused Houdini's death at Grace Hospital in Detroit, Michigan. He died in Room 401 located on Corridor D of the hospital. His death occurred on Halloween, October 31, 1926. He was buried in New York.

For further details on the life and times of Harry Houdini, take some time to visit your local library and see what you discover about this innovative individual who was a true master of magic. Harry Houdini continues to be revered as one of the greatest stage and public escape artists to ever live — and his ghost is seen in many locations throughout the world.

# Janesville

Founded in 1835, Janesville is a southern Wisconsin town on the bank of the Rock River. The city was named after Henry James, one of its early settlers.

A lynching in the downtown section in 1859 resulted in the ghost returning to haunt the site of its hanging, but these hauntings became less frequent with the passage of time. Some sightings have been in the city, reputed to be ghosts of early settlers. Other hauntings have appeared in the city's three cemeteries, with orbs seen during the night around grave markers.

The Lincoln-Tallman House is said to be haunted by the ghost of President Abraham Lincoln. The Hedberg Public Library is reputed to be haunted by a ghost of an older woman who appears in the restroom and then vanishes.

## Afterword
# GONE BUT NOT FORGOTTEN

There are settlements, villages, towns, mining sites, soldier camp sites, caves, abandoned haunted houses, and cemeteries which no longer exist for one reason or another, yet their existence is still remembered and their location is usually passed down by word of mouth. In attempting to compile such a list, it is necessary to talk to many people, and usually, each person has a different interpretation. This is a fine example of the Sociological Theory of Paradoxical Perception: Three people standing at three separate locations each witness an automobile accident, and when asked what they each saw, each one gives a different perspective on the details witnessed. Likewise, a site may have once been in a given area, but as to what is there now or a precise way for reaching it, that may be another story all together in trying to locate it.

If you are interested in ghost towns, compare old state or driving road maps to a new map.

Not all cemeteries are moved to a new location when faced with being permanently placed underwater. Why? Because not all sites may be remembered accurately as to precise location, or nobody remembers them. As a result, these burial sites are accidentally overlooked; this is nobody's fault.

Time does ironic things to human memories, as well as to where something is thought to be placed at any given setting in a landscape. Landscapes do not necessarily change, but where something is placed or buried on that designated landscape can, and do. When people abandon an area, they take their memories with them, and with the passage of time, those people and their memories are oftentimes sadly forgotten by those who come after them. There is no place truer for that than in the throwaway society of the USA, where one memory is quickly supplanted by new ones in the course of a day. So much is lost simply because there is so much to remember in our technological society!

The USA is constantly re-inventing itself as a nation, and that includes its history and memories of what went before. What is lost is lost, and that applies to historical sites. That loss is sad, and it is great, because there comes a reflective moment when all that is left is a keen feeling of nostalgia for those lost times, and words on paper to remind us of what we have lost. Americans too often destroy themselves by destroying their relics. America as a nation has forgotten now to preserve. For a society to destroy its relics through mishap or missed opportunity is to destroy its ability to leave a solid heritage for its descendants, and in many cases, that is what is happening in the USA today.

Just maybe, that is one of the numerous possible reasons why the living have ghosts, paranormal occurrences, and hauntings to remind them of some specific incident in the past. There are many ghosts around to remind the living, if only we would take the time to observe and learn the reasons why there are hauntings, and paranormal activity.

We are never alone. There will always be ghosts accompanying us on our journeys. For every living person, there are at least fifty ghosts waiting in line to talk with that person, or so the old saying goes. Yes, we are never alone.

# Glossary

**Ectoplasm**: A residue left behind by a ghost. Oftentimes ectoplasm is identified as having a misty or smoke-like quality about it.

**UFO (Unidentified Flying Object)**: Other terms include flying saucer, spacecraft, spaceship, unidentified submerged objects (going into or coming out of water), Interdimensional craft, black triangles, unidentified aerial phenomenon, ovni, saucer, alien spacecraft, flying disk, disk, disc, among many others.

**Ghost**: Also known as an apparition or spirit. A ghost is known by other names, such as phantom, specter, shade, wraith, revenant, and spook. A ghost is otherworldly and part of the community of the paranormal and supernatural. Ghosts may be female or male. A ghost when once alive in the flesh was an adult human, a human child, or an animal. Ghost appearances of pet companions are not uncommon.

**Intelligent Haunting**: This involves the appearance of a ghost in a given setting in which the ghost attempts to make itself known and contact the living around it.

**Orb**: A round ball of light connected with the presence of spirit energy. The ball may be of varying sizes. An orb is oftentimes seen by the naked eye and can be photographed. Orbs are also called Angel Lights.

**Paranormal**: Otherworldly, not of the living world. Paranormal activity is a form of existential reality based on pre-existing sequences in time.

**Paranormal Sensitive, or Sensitive**: Spelled either sensitive or Sensitive, this is an individual who can sense, see, hear, and talk with spirits or ghosts. The contemporary term, Paranormal Sensitive, is also used to identify such people with these natural gifts. The word comes from the old 1600s French, and means, literally, to see beyond the veil of death. Like psychics and mediums, a sensitive's gifts vary from

individual to individual. A sensitive usually does not make predictions or tell the future, although there are some who have developed those techniques.

**Portal**: An opening into an otherworldly setting, paranormal dimension, or supernatural location, through which an individual may enter for contact with otherworldly entities. A time portal is but one of several types of portals. Time portals may involve paranormal activity or a direct connection to UFO activity. Portals act upon space, time, and dimensions in ways not fully known or explained at this time in human history. No actual documentation of a person returning from a portal has ever been made.

**Residual Haunting**: This involves repeated appearances of a ghost in a given setting in which the ghost does not make contact with humans. Much like a tape recording, it simply repeats itself.

**Shadow Figure**: A figure that may have defined characteristics; it could be a human being or an animal. There are many theories about shadow figures; they may appear in daylight or at night, and may become solid, misty, or shadowy. A shadow figure may approach a living person or disappear at the approach of a living person. There have been reports of people being touched by shadow figures.

**Time loops, time slips, time blips, time portals**: An opening in time through which an individual may enter to view and/or connect with events. This applies to past events as well as future events. There are many approaches to achieving this, and numerous documented accounts of it taking place. *(See also portal)*

# Bibliography and Other Resources

Andrews, Ted. *How to Uncover Your Past Lives*. Woodbury, Minnesota: Llewellyn Publications, 2002.

Baldwin, Barbara J, Garretson, Jerri, Madl, Linda, and McGathy, Sherri L. *Trespassing Time: Ghost Stories from the Prairie*. Manhattan, Kansas: Ravenstone Press, 2005.

Belanger, Jeff. *Encyclopedia of Haunted Places*. Franklin Lakes, New Jersey: New Page Books, 2009.

*The Ghost Files*. Franklin Lakes, New Jersey: New Page Books, 2007.

*Ghosts of War: Restless Spirits of Soldiers, Spies, and Saboteurs*. Franklin Lakes, New Jersey: New Page Books, 2006.

*The Mysteries of the Bermuda Triangle*. New York, New York: Penguin Group, 2010.

*Communicating With the Dead: Reach Beyond the Grave*. Franklin Lakes, New Jersey: New Page Books, 2005.

*Our Haunted Lives: True Life Ghost Encounters*. Franklin Lakes, New Jersey: New Page Books, 2006

*The World's Most Haunted Places*. Franklin Lakes, New Jersey: New Page Books, 2004.

Berry, Earl. *Pioneer Life and Pioneer Families of the Ozarks*. Cassville, Missouri: Litho Printers, 1980.

Bruce, Robert & Mercer, Brian. *Mastering Astral Projection: 90-Day Guide to Out-of-Body Experience*. Woodbury, Minnesota: Llewellyn Publications, 2004.

Buckland, Raymond. *Buckland's Book of Spirit Communications, 2nd Edition*. Woodbury, Minnesota: Llewellyn Publications, 2004.

Budd, Deena West. *The Weiser Field Guide to Cryptozoology*. Newburyport, Massachusetts: Weiser, 2010.

Castaneda, Carlos. *The Wheel of Time*. New York, New York: Washington Square Press, 1998.

Churchill, Winston S. *The American Civil War*. London, England: Cassell & Company, 1961.

Churton, Tobias. *The Gnostics*. New York, New York: Barnes & Noble. 1997.

*Gnostic Philosophy*. Rochester, Vermont: Inner Traditions, 2005.

Cohen, Daniel. *Civil War Ghosts*. New York, New York: Scholastic, 1999.

Conway, D. J. *The Mysterious, Magickal Cat*. Woodbury, Minnesota: Llewellyn Publications, 1998.

Curran, Bob. *Encyclopedia of the Undead: A Field Guide to the Creatures That Cannot Rest in Peace*. Franklin Lakes, New Jersey: New Page Books, 2006.

Danelek, J. Allan. *The Case For Ghosts: An Objective Look at the Paranormal*. Woodbury, Minnesota: Llewellyn Publications, 2006.

Davidson, Wilma. *Spirit Rescue: A Simple Guide to Talking with Ghosts and Freeing Earthbound Spirits*. Woodbury, Minnesota: Llewellyn Publications, 2006.

Donovan, Timothy H. *The American Civil War*. Wayne, New Jersey and New York: Avery Publishing Group, 2000.

DuQuette, Lon Milo. *The Magick of Aleister Crowley*. York Beach, Maine: Weiser Books, 2003.

Dunwich, Gerina. *A Witch's Guide to Ghosts and the Supernatural*. Franklin Lakes, New Jersey: New Page Books, 2002.

*Dunwich's Guide to Gemstone Sorcery: Using Stones for Spells, Amulets, Rituals, and Divination*. Franklin Lakes, New Jersey: New Page Books, 2003.

*Phantom Felines and Other Ghostly Animals*. New York, New York: Citadel Press, 2006.

*Your Magickal Cat: Feline Magick, Lore, and Worship*. New York, New York: Citadel Press, 2000.

*The Concise Lexicon of the Occult*. New York, New York: Citadel Press, 1990.

Ebon, Martin. *They Knew The Unknown*. New York, New York: The World Publishing Company, 1971.

Eynden, Rose Vanden. *Ask A Medium*. Woodbury, Minnesota: Llewellyn, Minnesota Publications, 2010.

*So You Want to Be a Medium: A Down-to-Earth Guide*. Woodbury, Minnesota: Llewellyn Publications, 2006.

Feather, Fran Dancing, and Rita Robinson. *Exploring Native American Wisdom*. Franklin Lakes, New Jersey: New Page Books, 2003.

Filan, Kenaz. *The Haitian Vodou Handbook: Protocols for Riding with the Lwa*. Rochester, Vermont: Destiny Books, 2007.

Fiore, Edith. *The Unquiet Dead*. New York, New York: Dolphin, 1987.

Floyd, E. Randall. *In the Realm of Ghosts and Hauntings*. Augusta, Georgia: Harbor House, 2002.

Fodor, Nandor. *Between Two Worlds*. West Nyack, New York: Parker Publishing Company, 1964.

Gogh, Anson V. *Wayward Spirits & Earthbound Souls*. Woodbury, Minnesota: Llewellyn, 2010.

Goode, Caron B. *Kids Who See Ghosts*. Newburyport, Massachusetts: Weiser, 2010.

Gray-Cobb, Maiya & Geof. *Angels: The Guardians of Your Destiny*. Huntsville, Arkansas: Ozark Mountain Publishing, 2008.

Guiley, Rosemary Ellen. *The Encyclopedia of Ghosts and Spirits, 2nd Edition*. New York, New York: Checkmark Books, 2000.

Hardinge, Emma. *History of Modern Spiritualism*. New York, New York: University Books, 1970.

Harryman, Wilma Groves. *Ozark Mountain Girl*. Leawood, Kansas: Leathers Publishing, 1997.

Harvey, John. *Photography and Spirit*. London, England: Reaktion Books Ltd., 2007.

Hawes, Jason and Grant Wilson with Michael Jan Friedman. *Ghost Hunting: True Stories of Unexplained Phenomena from the Atlantic Paranormal Society*. New York, New York: Simon & Schuster, 2007.

Holzer, Hans. *Ghosts: True Encounters with the World Beyond*. New York, New York: Black Dog & Leventhal Publishers, 1997.
*Real Hauntings: America's True Ghost Stories*. New York, New York: Barnes & Noble, Inc., 1995.
*True Ghost Stories*. New York, New York: Dorset Press, 2001.
*Window to the Past: How Psychic Time Travel Reveals the Secrets of History*. New York, New York: Citadel Press, 1993.

Honigman, Andrew (editor). *My Proof of Survival: Personal Accounts of Contact with the Hereafter*. Woodbury, Minnesota: Llewellyn Publications, 2003.

Hill, Gary Leon. *People Who Don't Know They're Dead*. York Beach, Maine: Weiser Books, 2005.

Kachuba, John. *Ghosthunters: On the Trail of Mediums, Dowsers, Spirit Seekers, and Other Investigators of America's Paranormal World*. Franklin Lakes, New Jersey: New Page Books, 2007.

Kenyon, J. Douglas. *Forbidden History*. Rochester, Vermont: Bear & Company, 2005.
*Forbidden Religion*. Rochester, Vermont: Bear & Company, 2006.

Kitei, Lynne D. *The Phoenix Lights*. Charlottesville, Virginia: Hampton Roads Publishing, 2010.

Klinger, Sharon Anne. *Advanced Spirit Communication and Public Mediumship, 2nd Edition*. Westlake, Ohio: Starbringer Press, 2008.

Koltuv, Barbara Black. *The Book of Lilith*. Berwick, Maine: Nicolas-Hays, 1986.

Kubler-Ross, Elizabeth. *The Wheel of Life*. New York, New York: Scribner, 1997.

LeShan, Lawrence. *The Medium, the Mystic, and the Physicist*. New York, New York: Viking Press, 1974.

Leek, Sybil. *Reincarnation: The Second Chance*. New York, New York: Stein and Day, 1974.

Lowry, Thomas P. *The Stories the Soldiers Wouldn't Tell: Sex in the Civil War*. Mechanisburg, Pennsylvania: Stackpole Books, 1994.

Macy, Mark. *Spirit Faces: Truth About the Afterlife*. York Beach, Maine: Weiser Books, 2006.

Malachi, Tau. *Gnosis of the Cosmic Christ*. Woodbury, Minnesota: Llewellyn, 2005.

Marsh, Clint. *The Mentalist's Handbook: An Explorer's Guide to Astral, Spirit, and Psychic Worlds*. Newburyport, Massachusetts: Red Wheel/Weiser, 2008.

Martello, Leo Louis. *Witchcraft: The Old Religion*. New York, New York: Citadel Press, 1991.

Martinez, Susan B. *The Psychic Life of Abraham Lincoln*. Franklin Lakes, New Jersey: New Page Books, 2007.

McConnell, Kathleen. *Don't Call Them Ghosts: The Spirit Children of Fontaine Manse*. Woodbury, Minnesota: Llewellyn Publications, 2004.

McTeer, J. E.. *Fifty Years as a Low Country Witch Doctor*. Columbia, South Carolina: The R. L. Bryan Company, 1976.

Morehouse, David. *The Remote Viewing Training Course: Principles and Techniques of Coordinate Remote Viewing*. Boulder, Colorado: Sounds True, 2004.

Moroney, Jim. *The Extraterrestrial Answer Book: UFOs, Alien Abductions, and the Coming ET Presence*. Charlottesville, Virginia: Hampton Roads Publishing, 2009.

Moura, Ann. *Origins of Modern Witchcraft: The Evolution of a World Religion*. Woodbury, Minnesota: Llewellyn, 2000.

Morley, Christopher. *The Haunted Bookshop*. New York, New York: Barnes & Noble Books, 2004.

Nicholson, Shirley. *Shamanism*. Wheaton, Illinois: The Theosophical Publishing House, 1987.

Offutt, Jason. *Haunted Missouri: A Ghostly Guide to the Show-Me State's Most Spirited Spots*. Kirksville, Missouri: Truman State University Press, 2007.

Owens, Elizabeth. *Spiritualism & Clairvoyance for Beginners: Simple Techniques to Develop Your Psychic Abilities*. Woodbury, Minnesota: Llewellyn Publications, 2005.
   *How to Communicate with Spirits*. Woodbury Minnesota: Llewellyn Publications, 2001.

Price, Edwin. *Haints, Witches, and Boogers: Tales from Upper East Tennessee*. Winston–Salem, North Carolina: John F. Blair, Publisher, 1992.

Prosser, Lee. *Branson Hauntings*. Atglen, Pennsylvania: Schiffer Publishing, Ltd., 2010.

*Isherwood, Bowles, Vedanta, Wicca, and Me*. Lincoln, Nebraska: Writer's Club, 2001.

*Missouri Hauntings*. Atglen, Pennsylvania: Schiffer Publishing, Ltd., 2009.

*Night Tigers*. Lincoln, Nebraska: Writer's Club, 2002.

Rain, Mary Summer. *Eclipse*. Charlottesville, Virginia: Hampton Books, 1999.

*Soul Sounds*. Charlottesville, Virginia: Hampton Books, 1992.

Ramsland, Katherine. *Ghost: A Firsthand Account into the World of the Paranormal Activity*. New York, New York: St. Martin's Press, 2001.

Raven Wolf, Silver. *Mind of Light: Secrets of Energy, Magick & Manifestation*. Woodbury, Minnesota: Llewellyn Publications, 2006.

Redfern, Nick. *Contactees: A History of Alien-Human Interaction*. Franklin Lakes, New Jersey: New Page Books, 2010.

Ring, Kenneth and Evelyn Elsaesser Valarino. *Lessons from the Light: What we can Learn from the Near-Death Experience*. Needham, Massachusetts: Moment Point Press, 2000.

Rosa, Joseph G. *Age of the Gunfighter: Men and Weapons on the Frontier, 1840–1900*. Norman, Oklahoma: University of Oklahoma Press, 1995.

Schmitt, Jean Claude. *Ghosts in the Middle Ages: The Living and the Dead in Medieval Society*. Chicago, Illinois: University of Chicago Press, 1998.

Schnabel, Jim. *Remote Viewers: The Secret History of America's Psychic Spies*. New York, New York: Dell, 1997.

Silva, Freddy. *Secrets in the Fields*. Charlottesville, Virginia: Hampton Roads Publishing, 2010.

Slate, Joe H. *Beyond Reincarnation: Experience Your Past Lives & Lives Between Lives*. Woodbury, Minnesota: Llewellyn Publications, 2005.

Stavish, Mark. *Between the Gates: Lucid Dreaming, Astral Projection, and the Body of Light in Western Esotericism*. San Francisco, California: Weiser, 2008.

Steiger, Brad. *Real Ghosts, Restless Spirits, and Haunted Places*. Canton, Michigan: Visible Ink Press, 2003.

Stemman, Roy. *Spirits and Spirit Worlds*. New York, New York: Doubleday, 1963.

Tyson, Donald. *How to Make and Use a Magic Mirror: Psychic Windows Into New Worlds*. Custer, Washington: Phoenix Publishing, Inc., 1995.

Vaughan, Thomas. Edited by Arthur E. Waite. *Works of Thomas Vaughan, Mystic and Alchemist*. New Hyde Park, New York: University Books, 1969.

Wagner, Margaret E. *The American Civil War*. New York, New York: Harry N. Abrams, Inc., 2006.

Walter, Philippe. *Christianity: The Origins of a Pagan Religion*. Rochester, Vermont: Inner Traditions, 2003.

Watts, Alan. *In My Own Way: An Autobiography, 1915–1965*. Novato, California: New World, 2001.

Weisberg, Barbara. *Talking to the Dead: Kate and Maggie Fox and the Rise of Spiritualism*. New York, New York: Harper. 2004.

Wicker, Christine. *Lily Dale: The True Story of the Town That Talks to the Dead*. San Francisco, California: Harper, 2003.

Wilson, Colin. *Alien Dawn*. Woodbury, Minnesota: Llewellyn, 2010.

## INTERESTING WEBSITES

There are numerous Internet sites for ghost hunters in search of additional information and places of interest. With careful research, the reader will discover many, many more, including various organizations and universities that have some connection directly related to the paranormal, the supernatural, and ghosts.

Also remember to visit public libraries, state historical societies, local historical societies, newspapers, senior citizen organizations, folklore societies, and museums in your ongoing search for available information. You will be surprised with what you turn up in the course of a friendly conversation, or in reading! It may well lead you to overlooked ghost locations, hauntings, or paranormal activities waiting to be discovered by you!

There are ghosts out there, and you can discover them! I wish you personal good luck in compiling your own list of ghost hunting resources!

www.ghostvillage.com
www.theghostcatcher.com
www.ghosthunter.com
www.ghostsearch.org
www.ghoststore.net
www.hauntings.com
www.mindreader.com
www.ghosttowns.com
www.theshadowlands.net/ghost
www.nationalghosthunters.com/investigations.html
www.ghosts.net
www.prarieghosts.com
www.the-atlantic-paranormal-society.com
www.hollowhill.com
www.ghostweb.com
www.bransonghosttours.com

www.jeffdwyer.com
www.ispr.net/home.html
www.ghosthunting.com
www.annette-martin.com/
www.ghostweb.com
http://www.hauantedwriter.com/
http://www.para-x.com/
www.bransonghosttours.com
www.paranormalnews.com

## Images Credit

Sears Tower, Chicago © Stephen Finn; Lady Silhouette Blue Half Tone 2 © Tiffany Muff; Traveling over the Midwest © Jesse Kunerth; UFO © Iva Villi; Grunge Border and Background © Gordan Poropat, Airmail8 1963 and Arbor Day 1932 © Lawrence Long; Michigan Landmarks © Sreedhar Yedlapati; Sunset on a Lake in Minnesota © Andrew Tichovolsky; Welcome to Illinois © Katherine Welles; Wasbash River in Indiana © Alexey Stiop; Iowa Flag Close-up © Matt Trommer; Cave Background © Thomas Takacs; Civil War Statue © Craig Williams; Ghosts © Dejan Lazarevic; Welcome to Wisconsin © benkrut; and Open Door © Mike Tolstoy. *Courtesy of www.bigstockphoto.com.*

# INDEX